Principled Leader

ALSO BY KEVIN DOUGHERTY AND FROM MCFARLAND

The Vicksburg Campaign: Strategy, Battles and Key Figures (2015)

Military Decision-Making Processes: Case Studies Involving the Preparation, Commitment, Application and Withdrawal of Force (2014)

Military Leadership Lessons of the Charleston Campaign, 1861–1865 (2014)

The United States Military in Limited War: Case Studies in Success and Failure, 1945–1999 (2012)

BY KEVIN DOUGHERTY AND ROBERT J. PAULY, JR.

American Nation-Building: Case Studies from Reconstruction to Afghanistan (2017)

Principled Leadership

Theory and Case Studies

KEVIN DOUGHERTY

McFarland & Company, Inc., Publishers
Jefferson, North Carolina

LIBRARY OF CONGRESS CATALOGUING-IN-PUBLICATION DATA

Names: Dougherty, Kevin, author.
Title: Principled leadership : theory and case studies / Kevin Dougherty.
Description: Jefferson, North Carolina : McFarland & Company, Inc., Publishers, 2024 | Includes bibliographical references and index.
Identifiers: LCCN 2024007762 | ISBN 9781476694818 (paperback : acid free paper) ♾
ISBN 9781476652368 (ebook)
Subjects: LCSH: Leadership. | Leadership—Case studies.
Classification: LCC HD57.7 D684 2024 | DDC 658.4/092—dc23/eng/20240226
LC record available at https://lccn.loc.gov/2024007762

BRITISH LIBRARY CATALOGUING DATA ARE AVAILABLE

ISBN (print) 978-1-4766-9481-8
ISBN (ebook) 978-1-4766-5236-8

Printed in the United States of America

McFarland & Company, Inc., Publishers
Box 611, Jefferson, North Carolina 28640
www.mcfarlandpub.com

To Captain Geno Paluso
(United States Navy, Retired)
who as commandant of cadets
at The Citadel from 2014 to 2021
did much to model and advance
the cause of principled leadership.

Table of Contents

Preface

My interest in principled leadership stems from having held the position of assistant commandant for leadership programs at The Citadel. The Citadel is a senior military college in Charleston, South Carolina, with the mission "to educate and prepare graduates to become principled leaders in all walks of life by instilling the core values of The Citadel in a challenging intellectual environment."[1] The mission statement uses the expression "principled leader" very matter-of-factly, so when I first arrived on campus in 2010, I assumed there would be an abundance of literature awaiting me to answer my questions about this particular type of leader and leadership. I did, in fact, find much literature, but I did not find answers to my questions. Indeed, the more I read, the more questions I had.

The Citadel's general association of principles with leadership began in 1998 when Major General John Grinalds, college president from 1997 to 2005, declared that The Citadel should be "a model for preparing leaders in our society who are educated, responsible, and principled."[2] Beyond this pronouncement, General Grinalds did not expound on the term "principled" or how it would specifically characterize the type of leader or leadership he envisioned.

The term "principled leader" officially became part of The Citadel vernacular in 2003 when the *Cadet Academic Catalog* included it for the first time in the college vision and mission statements. The catalog stated that the college vision was "achieving excellence in the education of principled leaders" and the mission was "to educate and prepare graduates to become principled leaders in all walks of life by instilling the core values of The Citadel in a challenging intellectual environment."[3] In so doing, the 2003 catalog officially established principled leadership as The Citadel's leadership model of choice, but it presented no definition.

It was not until 2014 that The Citadel published a definition of principled leadership when *A Guide for the Leader Development Program* declared that "principled leadership is influencing others to accomplish organizational goals while adhering to the organization's core values."[4] This definition was revised in the 2017–2018 *Cadet Leader Development Program,* which states that principled leadership "is a form of value-based leadership ... [that] puts the leader's character into action, guiding thoughts, words, and deeds to produce outcomes consistent with the core values of the organization."[5]

As the assistant commandant for leadership programs, I was a member of the Leadership Development Council (LDC), a body established in 2013 by then–Citadel president Lieutenant General John Rosa to help guide leader development. In 2019, the LDC began work on a white paper designed to review the literature associated with principled leadership, record the evolution of principled leadership within The Citadel's leadership development model, and make recommendations for strengthening the theoretical and practical construct of principled leadership as a leadership style and The Citadel's use of it as a means of leader development. Working closely with Colonel Tom Clark, executive director of The Citadel's Krause Center for Leadership and Ethics, and Dr. Faith Rivers-James, chair of The Citadel's Department of Leadership Studies, our white paper quickly began to take shape. Over time, however, competing priorities and interests slowed progress. Certainly, one factor that made things difficult was the old adage that "the devil's in the details." The further we tried to move beyond the generalities and ambiguities we found permeating the literature and application of principled leadership, the harder it became to achieve consensus on those things that would truly make principled leadership a unique, robust, and distinctive style of leadership. We eventually placed the white paper on an indefinite hold.

Still, the project intrigued me, and I resolved to continue it on my own, even after I moved on from The Citadel. I began with the research question "What is principled leadership?" Building on what the white paper had taught me of the available literature and my own experience with principled leader development at The Citadel, I sought to answer this question by describing principled leadership in a way that specifically addressed each component of Peter Northouse's definition of leadership as "a process whereby an individual influences a group of individuals to achieve a common goal."[6] My hypothesis was that "in order for there to be something called 'principled leadership,' there must be principles that serve as the focus of the leader's actions." For my research methodology, I selected qualitative case studies using stratified sampling based on societal leadership roles such as business, military, and sports. Within the strata, I did some purposive sampling to ensure representation of various genders, races, and nationalities, but I leave it to and encourage future researchers to explore these populations as specific strata. If, as my hypothesis suggests, principles are universal, similar results should be expected. Armed with this research question, hypothesis, and methodology, I set out to write *Principled Leadership: Theory and Case Studies.*

My goal for the book is twofold. The first goal is to elevate principled leadership as a specific leadership style in terms of rigor and distinguishability. The Introduction targets this goal by attempting to answer the question "What is principled leadership?" The second goal is to champion its value by providing positive examples of its use. The book targets this goal by providing case studies drawn from business, political, military, religious, sports, literary, and societal leaders. The Conclusion summarizes points of commonality in the case studies and offers a short list of the "universal principles" recommended by them. This design is intended to appeal to readers interested in principled leadership both from academic and practical perspectives.

Introduction

What Is Principled Leadership?

Peter Northouse defines leadership as "a process whereby an individual influences a group of individuals to achieve a common goal."[1] If that is what leadership is in general terms, what, then, is the specific type of leadership known as "principled leadership"? Using Northouse's general definition of leadership as a guide, any understanding of principled leadership must include the following questions:

- What is the **definition** of principled leadership?
- How does the **process** of principled leadership work?
- How does a principled leader **influence** his or her followers?
- What is unique about the **goals** involved in a principled leadership environment?

A review of the existing literature addressing principled leadership reveals some answers to these questions but is also eclectic and incomplete, indicating the emergent nature of this particular leadership theory. Existing definitions of principled leadership are inexact and often more about the traits of the principled leader than principled leadership. Some authors have identified step-by-step processes for principled leadership, but they tend to be skeletons for what is obviously a more detailed process. In many cases, suggestions of the means a principled leader uses to influence seem indistinguishable from the means a leader using another leadership style would use. The goals in principled leadership would intuitively have something to do with principles, but the normative nature of values, the mixed vocabulary of values and principles, and the difficulty in agreeing on universal principles complicates the issue. Thus, while the extant literature is useful, it is only a starting point for what is a fledgling theory of leadership compared to more fully developed models such as transactional, transformational, and servant leadership. This state creates an exciting opportunity for scholars of principled leadership to make a meaningful contribution to the field. For the moment, let's review some of what has already been written in answer to our questions about principled leadership.

What Is the Definition of Principled Leadership?

A definition is "a statement expressing the essential nature of something."[2] "Essential nature" has an almost spiritual connotation to it. It is the quality or qualities that make a thing what it is. For a definition to capture something's essential nature, it must be precise, testable, clear, and distinguishable. Definitions of principled leadership that meet these criteria are elusive. Rather than define principled leadership, many authors instead adopt a trait approach to describe principled leaders. Oftentimes these traits seem indistinguishable from those of any good leader.

Karen Hendrikz and Amos Engelbrecht integrate transformational leadership, servant leadership, authentic leadership, and ethical leadership into "the construct of principled leadership." They then offer to define this "construct," but instead of defining "principled leadership," they describe what principled leaders are and what they do. Principled leaders, they write,

> inspire and motivate others with a sense of purpose that goes beyond their own needs and desires; they are trustworthy and act as role models of universally accepted moral behaviour by mastering their behaviour and interactions with others through humility, openness and vulnerability; by focusing on the empowerment of others and by being accountable for their own actions while holding others to account for theirs.[3]

In a book called *Principle-Centered Leadership*, one might expect to find a clearly stated definition of what author Stephen Covey describes as a "new paradigm."[4] He identifies levels, principles, and characteristics but never succinctly defines principle-centered leadership. Instead, he follows Hendrikz and Engelbrecht in defining the leader rather than the leadership style. Principle-centered leaders, Covey writes, "are men and women of character who work with competence 'on farms' with 'seed and soil' on the basis of natural principles and build those principles into the center of their lives, into the center of their relationships with others, into the center of their agreements and contracts, into their management processes, and into their mission statements."[5]

Writing in the context of the business environment, Manuel London defines both principled leadership and principled leaders. Principled leadership, he says, "is the application of ethical business values, including honesty, fairness, mutual respect, kindness, and doing good." Principled leaders, then, "are executives and managers who apply these values in their daily business lives."[6] While London's traits are obviously admirable, they do not seem to be particularly unique when compared to other leadership theories such as servant leadership or authentic leadership. London also uses the word "values" in his definition as opposed to Hendrikz and Engelbrecht and Covey who refer to "principles." Values and principles are not the same thing, and if the distinction is as stark as William Safire opines—that "principles are what you stand for in life; values are what you stand around in among your friends"[7]—then the word choice matters.

The Citadel has identified "principled leadership" as its signature brand of leadership since 2003 but did not offer a definition until 2014 when it declared that "principled leadership is influencing others to accomplish organizational goals while adhering to the organization's core values."[8] The Citadel follows London's example in discussing values rather than principles and offers a somewhat minimalistic definition. Requiring the leader to merely "adhere to" the organization's core values does not seem much to ask. Indeed, a leader who does not routinely adhere to the organization's core values would presumably find his or her stay in the organization a short one.

Because authors like London and The Citadel focus on values, it is useful to review Robert Daft's definition of "value-based leadership" as "a relationship between leaders and followers that is based on shared, strongly internalized values that are advocated and acted upon by the leader." In executing this form of leadership, value-based leaders "give meaning to activities and goals by connecting them to deeply held values."[9] Daft's definition seems to differ from those of principled leadership only in degree. For example, London requires principled leaders to "apply" their values, while Daft offers the perhaps slightly stronger admonition to "act" on them. Rather than merely "adhering" to the values as The Citadel's definition requires, Daft requires the leader to "advocate" for them. Covey expounds on how principle-centered leaders build principles into the "center" of things while Daft's value-based leaders "connect" things.

Value-based leadership has been the subject of scholarly inquiry since at least 2000 when Isaac Prilleltensky wrote an article intending "to introduce a model of value-based leadership." Even then, Prilleltensky began the article asking, "Do we not have enough models of leadership? Have we not talked enough about values in organizations? The answer to both questions is a qualified yes."[10] Of course, Prilleltensky proceeds to describe his new model and the parsing of leadership into increasingly nuanced elements seems to have, if anything, accelerated in recent years. Is there really a need for "principled leadership" as a separate and distinct leadership theory? If so, a unique definition that describes its "essential nature" is not readily apparent.

How Does the Process of Principled Leadership Work?

Michael Dantley notes that "principled leadership is demonstrated through reflective, ethical decision making, which is a process where principled leaders interrogate their motivation as well as the projected results of their decisions."[11] Like so much that is written about principled leadership, Dantley uses "loose coupling."[12] A careful reading of his sentence structure reveals that the "process" he refers to applies to "reflective, ethical decision making" rather than "principled leadership." In this case as in so many others, the reader feels he or she is close to principled leadership but can't quite touch it, let alone secure it in his or her grasp.

London does not identify a process for his version of "principled leadership and business diplomacy," but he does identify "process goals." These are:

— working together in the spirit of cooperation and, in the process, avoiding coercion, threat, and other negative interactions
— keeping communication open
— remaining flexible
— suggesting, and being open to, new ideas.[13]

London tells the reader what makes a principled leadership process a good one but leaves it to the reader to develop the process for himself or herself.

Maryann Glynn and Heather Jamerson provide a "framework for principled leadership," explaining that it "is not simply about having the right values or principles, but [is] also about being able to act on these principles when leaders find themselves in situations that may work against those principles and values."[14] They caution that it involves more than a basic understanding of and reflection on a decision-making process. Instead, principled leadership consists of an ongoing and intentional process of evaluating values against decisions and actions as they emerge. To facilitate this method, Glynn and Jamerson suggest a three-step principled leadership process of

1. awareness, making moral and ethical dimensions an explicit part of leadership decisions and action,
2. self-reflection on one's personal values, the firm's values, and their alignment, and
3. breathing life into organizations with principled leadership, using leadership skills of language, symbolism, and storytelling to enliven values.[15]

Their framework is "social and relational" and leads to actions that "overcome those situational factors that may challenge leaders' values and principles."[16]

In dealing with such challenges, James Kouzes and Barry Posner explain that options contrary to the leader's core values "are seldom considered or acted on; and if they are, it's done with a sense of compliance rather than commitment."[17] But Kouzes and Posner also introduce the notion that leadership based solely on values, no matter how desirable, is not always possible, and principled leaders cannot escape the ever-present tension between their principles and pragmatism. Similarly, Joseph Badaracco observes that

> principles alone qualify men and women to be preachers or saints. They can inspire and guide us, but usually don't make the trains run on time. Pure pragmatists can open their toolkits and go to work, but their amorality makes them dangerous.[18]

Although both characteristics are desired, Badaracco argues that "combining principles and pragmatism is among the most difficult challenges leaders face."[19] Principled leaders must recognize the situational context and work within it in a principled manner.

London agrees that "principled leaders are not Pollyannas" and that kindness and empathy are not the solutions to every challenging situation. He explains that while principled leaders apply values daily, they do not ignore harsh realities but rather "make difficult decisions, resolve conflicts, and negotiate deals" in keeping with values. In the context of business diplomacy, London argues that "principled leaders try to be fair and kind. Whether they do this out of the goodness of their hearts or because they believe that it is good business (or both) does not matter. What is important is that they act in a diplomatic way to make decisions, resolve conflict, and negotiate agreements."[20]

London's emphasis on the "diplomatic way" might be an example of the "backbone" Anna Simons contrasts with a "box" to describe how the process of principled leadership unfolds. She explains that a principle, like a backbone, represents an internalized structure, a deeply embedded set of core values and convictions that allow a leader "to operate anywhere; they don't have to think about what *not* to do; they know from within."[21] A box, in contrast, represents the absence of core values and convictions, resulting in the need for rules and regulations, which act as externally established constraints that delineate what is acceptable and what is not. The result is that principled leadership is a very empowering form of leadership that makes available to the leader a host of options, so long as they are consistent with the values. The principles lend the process the "consistency, resiliency, and strength" necessary to stay the course.[22] Lynn Paine offers a framework similar to that of Simons, explaining that once strategies that define the organization's "values, aspirations, and patterns of thought and conduct" are integrated organizationally, they serve to help prevent unethical decision-making, and over time, the ethical framework built on these strategies becomes "the governing ethos of an organization."[23]

This review of the existing literature of the process of principled leadership reveals many broad guidelines such as the importance of reflection, but to the degree that a process is "a series of actions or operations conducing to an end," specifics are few. Glynn and Jamerson's three-step process is a fledgling effort but begs for additional development. London and Badaracco realistically conclude that situational factors and pragmatics cannot be wished away, suggesting that absolute principled leadership may be an aspirational process. Simons and Paine also allude to the philosophical and organizational aspects of the process that would help to focus the effort and make it regenerative. In spite of these offerings, descriptions of the process of principled leadership remain generic and largely conceptual. In *Leading Change*, John Kotter identifies an eight-step process and then devotes over 100 pages to a step-by-step explanation of how the process works. No such in-depth model of the process of principled leadership exists.

How Does a Principled Leader Influence His or Her Followers?

According to Gene Klann, "influence is the application of power." Power itself is not the actual influencing action. It is merely the *capacity* to influence others, but Klann argues, "without power, there is little influencing; and with no influencing, there is no opportunity to gain genuine compliance or commitment from others."[24] "Leaders," he writes, "can use their power to affect and change the behaviors, values, attitudes, morale, and commitment level of those they lead."[25]

Klann examines six leadership styles. Unfortunately, principled leadership is not among them. Of the ones he discusses, he argues that the authoritative (not authoritarian) style of leadership is most effective in achieving outcomes of a positive climate, high levels of performance, and deeper follower commitment. In this style, leaders influence followers to achieve these outcomes by mobilizing people toward a common vision and embodying a "come with me" attitude. The leader enthusiastically works to get people on board with the vision. The leader focuses on follower ownership and energetically strives to get buy-in of the vision. Because of this, authoritative leaders usually have very effective communication skills.[26]

Gary Yukl and Cecilia Falbe report that there are two independent sources of power: position and personal.[27] Position power comes from the authority of the position held by the leader and promotes follower compliance. Personal power comes from the leader's followers and is based on their trust, admiration, and respect for the leader.[28]

According to Yukl, the application of a leader's power comes mainly through a variety of "influence tactics."[29] These can be grouped into the three broad categories of hard, soft, and rational tactics, and situational factors help determine which influencing tactic the leader will apply. Hard tactics are "generally used when the leader is expecting significant resistance, the leader or influencer has the upper hand, or when the person influenced violates the protocols of appropriate behavior with the leader."[30] Soft tactics are used when it is important to gain follower commitment, when the influencer is at somewhat of a disadvantage, when minor resistance is expected, or when the influencer will personally benefit if the influencing effort is a success.[31] Rational tactics are "generally used when the two parties are of equal rank or power, when no resistance is expected, or when both the organization and the influencer will benefit."[32]

Klann adds that leaders achieve results by either commitment- or compliance-focused influence. Compliance-focused influence is directed at follower behavior and is generally effective for gaining short-term and immediate results. It also works well in time-constrained environments with basic tasks that require a specific action or behavior and when there is little need for follower understanding.[33] Commitment is an outcome in which the follower agrees with direction from the leader and makes a strong effort to efficiently follow the direction. Compliance, on the other hand, is an outcome in which the follower is willing to do what the leader asks but lacks passion about it and makes only a token effort.[34] Hard tactics are compliance focused. Soft tactics are commitment focused. Rational tactics "initially appeal to compliance but can lead to commitment because they typically generate short-term wins that can, if consistently applied, sway the attitudes and beliefs of the followers or targets."[35]

The language of principled leadership tends toward "commitment" rather than "compliance." Covey, for example, speaks of "a commitment to a set of principles."[36] Following this inference, soft and rational tactics of influence would be more compatible with principled leadership than hard ones. This conclusion seems to be consistent with London's argument that "the main purpose of principled, diplomatic activity is to influence others."[37] In general terms, he advocates a "soft sell" approach that "provides buyers with information and helps them make a thorough analysis and reasoned, careful decision." "The hallmarks of principled leadership and business diplomacy," according to London, "are treating people with kindness and respect and enhancing communication and participation in achieving common goals." A "hard sell" approach, he writes, "puts many people off."[38]

Yukl and his colleagues identify nine "influence tactics" that agents use either individually or in combination.

Rational persuasion
Inspirational appeals
Consultation
Ingratiation
Personal appeals
Exchange
Coalition tactics
Pressure
Legitimizing tactics[39]

In the context of principled leadership, several seem inappropriate. These include ingratiation ("praise and flattery before or during an attempt to influence the target person to carry out a request or support a proposal"), personal appeals (asks "the target to carry out a request or support a proposal out of friendship, or asks for a personal favor before saying what it is"), exchange (offering "something the target person wants, or offers to reciprocate at a later time, if the target will do what the agent requests"), and pressure (using "demands, threats, frequent checking, or persistent reminders to influence the target to do something"). Inspirational appeals in which "the agent appeals to the target's values and ideals or seeks to arouse the target person's emotions to gain commitment for a request or proposal" seems the most compatible with principled leadership. Again, the emphasis is on "commitment" rather than "compliance."

In his study of the "psychology of compliance," Robert Cialdini identifies six "weapons of influence": reciprocation, consistency/commitment, social proof, liking, authority, and scarcity.[40] Cialdini's is a cautionary tale of what a manipulative and double-edged sword influence can be. Some of Cialdini's weapons can intuitively be seen as dangerous to principled leadership. "Liking," for example, he describes as "the friendly thief."[41] Others are a little more insidious, especially as responses to them become more mechanical and automatic. For example, while obedience to authority is "mostly rewarding," mindless obedience, Cialdini cautions, means "we don't have to think, therefore we don't."[42] Similarly, our tendency toward consistency is strong enough to make us do things that we ordinarily would not want to do.[43] Cialdini provides the reader valuable warning as to how influence can be used in an unprincipled way, especially when the emphasis is on compliance rather than commitment.

Whereas Yukl and Cialdini's lists are not specific to any particular leadership theory, Covey offers "thirty means of influence" in the context of principle-centered leadership.

1. Refrain from saying the unkind or negative thing, particularly when you are provoked or fatigued.
2. Exercise patience with others.
3. Distinguish between the person and the behavior or performance.

4. Perform anonymous service.
5. Choose the proactive response.
6. Keep the promises you make to others.
7. Focus on the circle of influence.
8. Live the law of love.
9. Assume the best of others.
10. Seek first to understand.
11. Reward open, honest expressions or questions.
12. Give an understanding response.
13. If offended, take the initiative.
14. Admit your mistakes, apologize, ask for forgiveness.
15. Let arguments fly out open windows.
16. Go one-on-one.
17. Renew your commitment to things you have in common.
18. Be influenced by them first.
19. Accept the person and the situation.
20. Prepare your mind and heart before you prepare your speech.
21. Avoid fight or flight—talk through differences.
22. Recognize and take time to teach.
23. Agree on the limits, rules, expectations, and consequences.
24. Don't give up, and don't give in.
25. Be there at the crossroads.
26. Speak the languages of logic and emotion.
27. Delegate effectively.
28. Involve people in meaningful projects.
29. Train them in the law of the harvest.
30. Let natural consequences teach responsible behavior.[44]

Covey touts that these methods will "powerfully and ethically influence the lives of other people."[45] Indeed, in many aspects Covey's list seems to be sound interpersonal advice about how to treat people. He has definitely expounded on the Golden Rule and much of his wisdom is transferrable to principled leadership, but he does not always tightly couple his recommendations for how to influence with the tangible results demanded of a leader.

Such coupling is essential. Leadership is of course relational, but the purpose of influence in the context of leadership is, according to Northouse, to get individuals "to achieve a common goal"[46] rather than Covey's more general purpose of merely influencing "the lives of other people." In the context of leadership, relational influence is a means, not an end. For example, in explaining the "law of love," Covey writes, "We can gain even greater influence with [people] by showing love, particularly unconditional love, as this gives people a sense of intrinsic worth and security unrelated to conforming behavior or comparisons with others."[47] Even though this is beautiful sentiment, few leaders who have the duty to accomplish the goals required of them can afford to operate without placing conditions such as "conforming behavior" on their followers.

Ruth Bernheim and Alan Melnick address this need for conforming behavior, arguing that in a principled leadership environment, "officials committed to incorporating ethics into practice must create an organizational context within their agencies that is grounded in ethics. This could be accomplished by tying employee-performance standards to ethical principles and by encouraging staff to integrate ethics into their daily work by developing goals, objectives, and measurable outcomes that are based on ... values and principles."[48] Writing specifically about the field of public health, Bernheim and Melnick offer a 12-item list of "The Principles of the Ethical Practices of Public Health" as a "systematic means" and "systematic guidance" to "use the same principles consistently when deliberating about various decisions."[49]

Given the centrality of influence in leadership—Northouse opines that "without influence, leadership does not exist"[50]—one would expect to find somewhere in the principled leadership scholarship direct statements along the lines of "principled leaders influence by...." This review revealed nothing so definitive. However, certain themes do emerge including the preference to influence by commitment rather than compliance, the use of soft rather than hard tactics, and a reliance on personal more than position power. The type of influence exerted by authoritative leaders that emphasizes vision, unity, involvement, ownership, and communication seems to have some transferability to principled leadership.

What Is Unique About the Goals Involved in a Principled Leadership Environment?

After identifying "process goals" for principled leadership and business diplomacy, London offers the following "outcome goals":

- achieving positive outcomes
- aiming for unanimity (or at least arriving at a consensus)
- pursuing stable agreements
- improving interpersonal competencies
- establishing a team identity
- fostering positive relationships to navigate future dilemmas, disagreements, and deals[51]

London adds that "the results of the diplomatic effort can be measured against these goals. That is, were the goals accomplished?"[52] London appears to be using "goals" slightly differently than how the word is used in leadership definitions such as Northouse's. In Northouse's sense, goals are the desired objectives, outcomes, end state, or results. London's "goals" appear to be the criteria used to access the manifestation of those desired objectives, outcomes, end state, or results. In this context, London's goals are certainly compatible with the soft influence tactics he champions.

Although London insists on "positive" outcomes, he does not explicitly state what constitutes a positive outcome. Elsewhere he suggests it has something to do with "everyone [being] pleased with the end result," "everyone leaving [with the] feeling they had achieved an important part of their goal," and "participants compromis[ing]."[53] It is easy to imagine how such considerations, especially compromise, might result in a deviation from pure principles.

Instead of London's emphasis on fostering continued relationships and goodwill, it seems intuitive that the goals involved in a principled leadership environment would be closely correlated with the leader's principles and values. Some of the definitions examined earlier support this assumption, such as The Citadel's definition that "principled leadership is influencing others to accomplish organizational goals while adhering to the organization's core values." Upon closer study, however, the clause "while adhering to the organization's core values" seems to modify how the leader "influences others" rather than the "goals." As with many aspects of principled leadership, understanding what might be unique about the goals is not directly addressed in the literature. Part of that indirectness may have something to do with the difference between values and principles.

Principled leadership is a form the "ethical leadership" that Michael Brown and his colleagues define as "the demonstration of normatively appropriate conduct through personal actions and interpersonal relationships, and the promotion of such conduct to followers through two-way communication, reinforcement, and decision-making."[54] Like all things "normative," then, what is deemed "appropriate conduct" is determined by the overall society or some subset of the society. One variable in this determination are the values of the society or subset.

Bill George writes that values represent "the relative importance of the things that matter" in life.[55] Of immediate note is that George speaks of values in the *relative* rather than *absolute* context. His description also poses the immediate question of "matter to whom?" Indeed, many organizations select values to serve as social norms of the organization, and like all values, they tend to be personal, emotional, subjective, and arguable.[56] They describe the behavior that is accepted by consensus in the organization and the values become central to each member's social acceptance.[57] Values are unique to the given organization, but all organizations, even criminal, hateful, and selfish ones, have some type of behavior that they value and embrace.[58]

But in the context of principled leadership, values are based on principles. William Safire notes that "principle" comes from the Latin *principium*, meaning "source, origin, beginning," and on that basis the word "came to mean a primary truth that formed the basis for other beliefs and then to mean a rule for ethical conduct."[59] Covey declares principles to be "impersonal, factual, objective, and self-evident." According to Covey, principles transcend other factors in that even though different cultures may translate principles into different practices and the wrongful use of freedom may obscure principles over time, the principles remain. He equates them to natural laws that operate constantly.[60] David Guralnik, editor of Webster's *New World Dictionary*, seemingly agrees, explaining that "principles, being theological in origin, are fixed, invariable, absolute, eternal. Values, being in a sense scientific, are nontheological and therefore subject to change and alteration as the demands and needs of a society change."[61] Covey continues that values may govern behavior, but principles govern consequences, and his principle-centered leadership aims to align the organization's values with nature's changeless principles.[62]

Principles enable leaders to focus on something objective. Ken Shelton opines that "real leadership development begins with the humble recognition that principles ultimately govern." He observes that when most people talk about ethics and values, they refer to personal beliefs and situational behaviors, not universal principles and natural laws, which, like Covey, he argues are objective and absolute. Because Shelton believes that few people consider universal values but rather focus on the things they individually value, he contends that it typically takes an organizational or personal crisis for leaders to subordinate their values to universal principles.[63]

Hendrikz and Engelbrecht also identify "the need to move away from moral relativism towards universally recognized moral principles, if behavior is to be judged as either ethical or unethical."[64] The question then becomes "What are these universal principles?" Unfortunately, these universal principles are frequently referred to in concept but seldom enumerated.

Hendrikz and Engelbrecht offer a list drawn from an "analysis of the sacred texts of the major religions of the world, codes of secular organizations that focus on morality..., corporate codes of ethics and business ethics literature." These "universal moral values" are:

1. Commitment to something greater than oneself
2. Trustworthiness
3. Respect for self, human race, the environment, and other living beings
4. Responsibility
5. Fairness

6. Caring
7. Citizenship[65]

To get their list, Hendrikz and Engelbrecht combined a list generated by Richard Kinnear, Jerry Kernes, and Therese Dautheribes in 2000[66] with another generated by Mark Schwartz in 2005.[67] Merely combining two lists does not intuitively seem definitive, and the list is also of values rather than principles.

Louis Pojman and James Fieser offer 10 "principles necessary for the good life within a flourishing human community." These "examples of the core morality" are:

1. Do not kill innocent people.
2. Do not cause unnecessary pain or suffering.
3. Do not lie or deceive.
4. Do not steal or cheat.
5. Keep your promises and honor your contracts.
6. Do not deprive another person of his or her freedom.
7. Do justice, treating people as they deserve to be treated.
8. Reciprocate: Show gratitude for services rendered.
9. Help other people, especially when the cost is minimal.
10. Obey just laws.[68]

Note the difference between a list of values and a list of principles. Hendrikz and Engelbrecht's list of values are one-word concepts. Pojman and Fieser's principles are statements directing specific action. Interesting, though, is the fact that their principles are equally split between positives and negatives. Not doing something bad certainly is not the same as doing something good, and it would seem that principles that promote a certain positive action would be more powerful than principles that merely prohibit a certain negative action. Knowing what not to do still leaves the actor with the problem of determining what to do.

Using slightly different and more guarded language, Oliver Curry, Daniel Austin Mullins, and Harvey Whitehouse provide a list of "seven cooperative behaviors [that] are plausible candidates for universal moral rules." These are "helping kin, helping your group, reciprocating, being brave, deferring to superiors, dividing disputed resources, and respecting prior possession."[69] Although these behaviors are all positive, Curry and his colleagues do not propose how to move from plausible candidacy to universal acceptance.

Kent Keith offers a "universal moral code" made up of "fundamental moral principles that can be found throughout the world." Like Pojman and Fieser, he lists his code in a negative and a positive format. The "do no harm" list is:

> Do not do to others what you would not like them to do to you.
> Do not lie.
> Do not steal.
> Do not cheat.
> Do not falsely accuse others.
> Do not commit adultery.
> Do not commit incest.
> Do not physically or verbally abuse others.
> Do not murder.
> Do not destroy the natural environment on which all life depends.

Keith's "do good" list is:

> Do to others what you would like them to do to you.
> Be honest and fair.
> Be generous.
> Be faithful to your family and friends.
> Take care of your children when they are young.
> Take care of your parents when they are old.
> Take care of those who cannot take care of themselves.
> Be kind to strangers.
> Respect all life.
> Protect the natural environment on which all life depends.[70]

Although Keith's effort is admirable, it quickly runs into trouble when measured against universal application. If by "throughout the world" Keith means "everywhere" or "in every part of," then it is easy to find exceptions on the list. Adultery, for example, is illegal in less than half of the states in the United States, and many a refugee might wonder at the universality of "be kind to strangers."

Introduction

This brief survey of various attempts to provide a set of universal principles is of course an exercise in the obvious. There is no one list of principles on which the entire universe agrees. Moral absolutists certainly agree that such universal principles exist, but the search for what they may be continues. That appears problematic if principled leadership is to be based on something more than normative values, yet without principles, it seems intuitively obvious that there can be no "principled" leadership.

Moving Forward

This discussion began with the premise that using Northouse's general definition of leadership as a guide, any understanding of principled leadership must include:

— What is the **definition** of principled leadership?
— How does the **process** of principled leadership work?
— How does a principled leader **influence** his or her followers?
— What is unique about the **goals** involved in a principled leadership environment?

The review of the literature did not generate consistent, decisive, and detailed answers to these questions, but it did reveal some general themes. The following is an attempt to add rigor and specificity to those themes.

Definition

Principled leadership is the process of using principles as the means of influencing others to accomplish goals that optimize those principles, even at the expense of other considerations.

Process

Two processes seem to be required. The first is to determine the organization's principles and infuse them in the organization, its leaders, and its members. The second is the subsequent application of those principles in a given situation. The endnotes for each step refer to the basis of that step as found in existing literature.

Process 1: Determining and Infusing the Principles

1. Develop an understanding of the organization's values. This should tell you what is important to the organization.[71]
2. Develop or confirm your values. This should tell you what is important to you.[72]
3. Resolve any conflicts between your values and the organization's values.[73]
4. Develop a list of principles that serve as the framework for a systematic means of considering, deciding, communicating, measuring, and assessing leadership actions.[74]
5. Build organizational commitment to and alignment with the principles.[75]
6. Train the organization on the use of the principles.[76]
7. Regularly assess organizational culture and climate relative to the principles.[77]

Process 2: Applying the Principles

1. Gather the facts relevant to the situation.[78]
2. Review the statements of the principles.[79]
3. Determine what principles impact on or are impacted by this situation.[80]
4. Eliminate all solutions that are inconsistent with the principles.[81]
5. Determine if there is a hierarchy of principles in this situation.[82]
6. Determine what leader action is necessary (e.g., decide, issue a statement, provide guidance or instruction).[83]
7. Develop potential solutions that are consistent with the principles, especially those principles high on the hierarchy.[84]
8. Analyze each potential solution in the context of the principles and determine the relative advantages and disadvantages.[85]
9. Select the solution that best optimizes the principles, with special emphasis on those principles high on the hierarchy.[86]

10. If the solution involves some ambiguity, friction, or compromise, determine how to mitigate that risk. Included in this step is an accounting of those consequences that may result from optimization of principles, such as economic costs. Although not part of the principled leadership decision-making process, these consequences are real and must be reckoned with.[87]
11. Reflect on the process.[88] Ideally, write a brief synopsis that clearly states how you handled each step. If appropriate, solicit feedback from trusted advisers, empowering them to act as devil's advocates.[89] Make any adjustments necessary.
12. Initiate the action. To the fullest extent practical, explain the why to all stakeholders in terms of the principles.[90]

Influence

Transactional leaders influence by transactions. Authoritarian leaders influence by authority. Delegative leaders influence by delegating. Servant leaders influence by serving. Transformational leaders influence by transforming. Charismatic leaders influence by charisma. It seems obvious, then, that principled leaders influence by principles.

To influence, leaders establish a system. Transactional leaders establish a system of exchanges. Authoritarian leaders establish a system of hierarchical position power. Delegative leaders establish a system of empowerment. Principled leaders, then, must establish a system of principles. Like all leaders, they develop and share a vision, and the principled leader's vision must be of actions based on principles. Anna Simons argues that principled leadership is the opposite of proscriptive leadership in which the leader bases leadership decisions and actions on a set of rules, procedures, or other directives,[91] but aren't principles a form of rules? To be sure, in principled leadership, the principles are rules based on values rather than any other criteria or expediency, but they are still rules.

The influence of the principled leader seems to be front loaded. He or she must decide what the principles are, communicate them to his or her followers, establish philosophical alignment by dialogue, and then establish practical alignment by training. The advantage of the principles is that they provide overall guidance that can then be tailored to specific situations. There is no need to examine every single situation from scratch. The leader, the organization, and the members have all precommitted to the principles, and they conduct themselves accordingly, always. The leader continues to influence by example, reinforcement, and reflection, but once the ball is rolling, it is largely the principles themselves that provide the influence rather than an individual leader. When working correctly, influence in an organization devoted to principled leadership should be very organic, logical, and self-sustaining.

Goals

We will begin with the assumption that principled leadership and value-based leadership are not the same thing. What, then, is the difference in the goals of the two leadership models? The review of the literature clearly indicates that principles are stronger and more demanding than values. Values are subjective. Principles are objective. Values are normative. Principles are factual. Values are personal. Principles are impersonal. Values are qualities. Principles are rules. Values are changeable. Principles are changeless. Values are what we hold dear, and based on those values, principles govern our actions. In sum, a principle is "a comprehensive and fundamental law, doctrine, or assumption" or "a rule or code of conduct."[92]

The problem is that although universal principles may exist, there is no consensus on what they are, rendering the point rather moot from the standpoint of principled leadership. But if universal consensus is unattainable, to be of use for this purpose, what we do consider principles must be legitimate at the highest level of society possible, and to be legitimate, they must be stated.[93] This is often not the case.

Consider the example of The Citadel which declares its "most recognizable leadership brand" to be "a form of values-based leadership called principled leadership."[94] The Citadel explains that from its "longstanding history and deeply embedded traditions have emerged the institution's three core values: honor, duty, and respect."[95] "Principled leadership," The Citadel says, "puts the leader's character into action."[96] All this is good, but something is missing. There is no statement of what The Citadel's principles are. The progression must be from values to principles to actions. Without a clear statement of the principles, the leader must jump from values to actions. There is nothing inherently wrong with that, but there is also nothing inherently different between that model and value-based leadership. It seems that for "principled leadership" to really be something unique, at a minimum, the principles must be stated.

CADRE is a community-based, membership parent organization in South Los Angeles founded in 2001. They don't claim to be "principled leaders," but their statement of "beliefs, values, and principles" give us a good example of how values inform principles. CADRE lists a set of beliefs that "form the basis of everything we do." They believe, for example, that "every parent or caregiver in South LA is a valuable asset of the community." "Because of these beliefs," CADRE is able to list the things they "most value." Among them is "parent leadership development and power." Then CADRE moves from values to principles, declaring, "so that our work consistently reflects our beliefs and values, we operate with the following principles" and then lists principles such as "We strive for a membership equally balanced among African American and Latino parents, regardless of the demographics of schools and out of deep respect for both the shared and distinct histories and experiences in South LA."[97] CADRE lists its values, like value-based leadership, would require, but then it states how those values translate into operational principles. CADRE's principles are not universal to all humanity, but they are universal within their organization and are made legitimate by being written down. That seems to be a good practical model for any organization aspiring to lead by principled leadership. CADRE's beliefs, values, and principles are recorded in Appendix 1.

Case Studies

"God grant that men of principles shall be our principal men."—Thomas Jefferson

The following case studies provide examples of principled leadership. In all of the case studies, more than one principle and more than one lesson are present, but at the beginning of each case study a principle and lesson are identified as being of particular significance. The case studies are presented in groups representing business, political, military, religious, and societal leaders. References to material from the Introduction are made as appropriate, and a summary of points of commonality in the case studies is captured in the Conclusion.

Business Leaders

James Burke and the Tylenol Recall

Principle: "Put the needs and well-being of the people we serve first."[1]

Lesson: Once an organizational culture of principled leadership is established, the system largely runs itself.

The main way a principled leader influences is by the initial determination of the principles, communicating them to his or her followers, establishing philosophical alignment by dialogue, and then ensuring practical alignment by training. Once this preliminary work has been accomplished, principled leadership operates as a self-sustaining, logical, and organic part of the organization. An example of this aspect of principled leadership is how James Burke used it as CEO of Johnson & Johnson in response to the 1982 Tylenol poisoning crisis.

The basis of Johnson & Johnson's corporate principles comes from Robert Wood Johnson, a member of the company's founding family and its chairman from 1932 to 1963, who crafted the Johnson & Johnson "credo" in 1943. The company website summarizes the credo as challenging "us to put the needs and well-being of the people we serve first." According to the credo, the company is responsible first to its customers, then to its employees, the community, and the stockholders, in that order. "The values that guide our decision-making," the introduction continues, "are spelled out in Our Credo."[2] Burke became CEO of Johnson & Johnson in 1976 and quickly embarked on a campaign to make the credo the heart of the corporate culture.

Before becoming CEO, Burke was president of Johnson & Johnson, and he discovered a rather lackadaisical attitude toward the credo in many sectors of the company.[3] As one labor leader told him, "We talk about the Credo but a lot of our people aren't behaving by it." Burke knew that merely having a code was not enough. As Rushworth Kidder observed, "Enron, after all, had its elegant, full-color, sixty-four-page *Enron Code of Ethics* on its shelves during the period of its most egregious frauds."[4] In fact, the same Enron executives who included in the code a prohibition against off-the-books financial deals convinced the board of directors to waive that restriction.[5]

Burke decided to resolve the inconsistency between code and conduct at Johnson & Johnson by a series of high-level "challenge" meetings in which executives wrestled with the decision to live by or abandon the credo. "If it doesn't mean anything," Burke explained, "we should really come to that conclusion and tear it off the walls because it's an act of pretension to leave it up." In 1979, he brought together the company's global management and challenged them to increase the practical relevance of the credo within their organizations.

In September 1982, the first of seven people died in the Chicago area after consuming Tylenol capsules that had been laced with cyanide by an unknown perpetrator. Harvard Business School professor

Laura Nash notes that "*from an economic and public relations standpoint, one could have made a very reasonable argument for keeping the product on the shelves*: The contamination was not the company's fault, and did not appear to have originated from a J & J facility; this was an isolated incident, the result of aberrant behavior; the benefits of the product to the majority of the public vastly outweighed the injuries that might occur if the product remained on the shelves."[6] Nonetheless, Burke acted swiftly, ordering the withdrawal of Tylenol from store shelves everywhere, not just in the Chicago area. While admitting the $100 million recall placed a serious financial burden on the company, Burke notes the decision "was made not only simple but there wasn't anything else I could have done. Every person who worked for Johnson & Johnson in the world was watching the poisoning.... If we had done anything other than what we did, think about how those employees would have felt.... I mean, the very soul of the corporation was watching us."

As the events unfolded, "hundreds of people made thousands of decisions," and Burke reports "those thousands of decisions all had a splendid consistency about them and that was that the public was going to be served first." "The Credo," he says, "ran that because the hearts and minds of the people who were Johnson & Johnson and were making the decisions in a whole series of disparate companies—we organized every company in the United States to help solve the problem—they all knew what to do." Kidder reports that "when the time came for rapid-fire decision making up and down the corporate line ... the credo, and the commitment of the chairman to its implementation, was understood to be the standard."[7] For this reason, Lynn Paine concludes "the 'Tylenol decision,' then, is best understood not as an isolated incident, the achievement of a lone individual, but as a reflection of an organization's culture."[8] It is an example of how ethical values "provide a common frame of reference and serve as a unifying force across different functions, lines of business, and employee groups."[9]

Burke notes that the groundwork for this positive outcome was laid by the credo. "All the previous management who built this corporation handed us a silver platter in the most powerful tool you could possibly have." The internalization of the credo had established a culture of "This is the way we think and behave, and we won't tolerate behavior different than that." According to Burke, "having a corporate ethic, a corporate set of principles, a corporate soul if you will, makes it easier." Paine would seemingly agree, noting that "when integrated into the day-to-day operations of an organization, such strategies can help prevent damaging ethical lapses while tapping into powerful human impulses for moral thought and action. Then an ethical framework becomes no longer a burdensome constraint within which companies must operate, but the governing ethos of an organization."[10]

Rather than being restrictive, Burke found the corporate principles to be expanding. "I have no question in my mind that the Credo is a document that liberates creativity," he reports. "It helps people to do things better than they would do if it wasn't there because they aren't hamstrung by thinking what is expected of me. 'Do I have to cheat to deliver profits?' That's a very good question. The document suggests you better not. What the Credo says is you better understand your customer in exquisite detail." So long as a Johnson & Johnson member is operating within that framework, many options are available.

In a study of "what you can learn from the top 25 business people of our times," Mukul Pandya highlights Burke as providing "the most prominent—and by now legendary—example of good crisis management."[11] On one level, the crisis was in 1982 when the poisonings occurred, but on a much deeper level it was in the 1970s when Burke forced the company to resolve its ambiguity toward the credo. Once that initial crisis was resolved, subsequent crises had a frame of reference that allowed for the practice of principled leadership. As one manager recalled, the Tylenol crisis "was the tangible proof of what top management had said at the credo challenge meetings. You came away saying, *'My God! You're right. We really do believe this. It's for real. And we did what was right.'*"[12]

The Introduction of this book notes that there are two processes associated with principled leadership. The first is to determine the organization's principles and infuse them in the organization, its leaders, and its members. Burke did this by aligning Johnson & Johnson with its credo. The second process is the subsequent application of those principles in a given situation. Because Burke had done such a good job with the first process, the second process largely unfolded of its own accord. Such an outcome was not unique to the Tylenol crisis. It was the culture that Burke had created. As Brian Perkins, who at the time of the poisonings was a product director with McNeil Consumer Products, the Johnson & Johnson subsidiary that was the maker of Tylenol, recalled, "Whenever we were faced with a really hard decision, [Burke] would always point to the credo for guidance."[13] In so doing, Burke demonstrates the idea that the influence of a principled leader is largely front loaded.

John Hall and the Ashland Oil Spill

Principle: Take responsibility for and fix your mistakes.

Lesson: When an organization finds itself out of alignment with its principles, restore alignment as directly as possible.

What does a principled leader do when he finds himself in a situation where he or his organization is in violation of their principles? Whether the violation occurred through commission or omission, malice aforethought or mistake, design or surprise, the principled leader's response must be to as directly as possible restore alignment with the principles. John Hall's crisis response to the Ashland Oil Spill is an example of a principled leader taking such decisive action.

The Ashland Oil disaster occurred on January 2, 1988, when a tank holding some three and a half million gallons of diesel oil at the Floreffe terminal outside of Pittsburgh, Pennsylvania, collapsed. Nearly a million gallons of oil were dumped into a storm sewer that led to the Monongahela River, and from there, the oil spread into the Ohio River, ultimately contaminating the drinking water of some one million people in three states. It was the largest inland oil spill in U.S. history.

The stress generated from crises such as the Ashland Oil spill poses unique challenges to the human nature of the principled leader. Stress interferes with cognitive abilities, leading individuals to perceive the world less accurately and ignore or misinterpret important information. Organizations under stress tend to delegate decision-making to a small group of key officials, which may limit access to alternate perspectives and promote groupthink. Time restrictions and public scrutiny may make careful deliberation impossible and create pressure to act without adequate preparation.[14] Hall rose above these and other challenges to handle this crisis in a principled way.

Hall had been with Ashland since 1957 when he accepted a position as assistant to the coordinator of research and development. He steadily advanced through the ranks, holding positions in chemicals, refining, production, distribution, and management until he became the chairman and CEO in September 1981. Lynn Perry Wooten and Erika Hayes James point to the agility created by a leader who "understands all aspects of the organization and is able to span organizational boundaries to get things done" as one characteristic that is conducive to successful crisis management.[15] In this case, Hall's extensive background made him very familiar with all aspects of Ashland, and he was able to quickly grasp the magnitude of the situation.

Hall was informed of the spill at about nine the morning after it happened. By then, a crisis management team had been formed and was readying to fly to the site. At this point, Hall knew he faced a major environmental problem, but he felt that the Ashland personnel at and heading to Pittsburgh were sufficient to handle the immediate logistical requirements. He spent the morning of January 3 in his office, keeping in contact with the team at the Floreffe terminal, gathering information, authorizing expenditures to hasten the cleanup, and developing the plan to minimize the spill's impact.[16]

At Floreffe, however, efforts to contain the spill proved ineffective, and the situation continued to worsen. Oil flowing downriver forced the Western Pennsylvania Water Company, which supplied part of the drinking water used by suburban Pittsburgh, to shut down one of its facilities. This new possibility of water shortages elevated the crisis to yet another level, and Hall directed Ashland to pay for a temporary pipe to secure fresh water from the Allegheny River. He also authorized funds to fly in the Coast Guard Strike Force on Air Force C5A transport planes to expedite cleanup operations. That evening, he telephoned Governor Bob Casey of Pennsylvania and Governor Arch Moore of West Virginia to apologize for the situation and to assure them that Ashland was working to improve it.[17]

Once an individual recognizes an ethical issue exists, the Markkula Center for Applied Ethics at Santa Clara University identifies "get the facts" as the next step in its "A Framework for Ethical Decision Making."[18] "Everywhere I looked," Hall later said about his effort to get the facts, "we had done something wrong."[19] The tank had not been hydrostatically tested as directed by American Petroleum Standard 650, the industry guidelines for proper testing of oil tanks. Construction had been started based on verbal communication rather than an approved permit. The application for the permit failed to mention that the tank was to be rebuilt from 40-year-old steel.[20] "The further I dug," Hall recalled, "the madder I got."[21]

Craig Johnson lists "demonstrate care and concern" as one of the "components of ethical crisis management."[22] A leader's physical presence is one way to demonstrate care and concern, and on the morning of January 5, Hall flew to Pittsburgh. Daryl Koehn notes that "Hall's willingness to meet these injured individuals in their hometown testified to his desire to know exactly what was going on and to show solidarity with the victims of the spill." "This choice of venue," Koehn continues, "reinforced his message that the company would make things right."[23]

Although there was little Hall could do physically in terms of cleanup operations, his personal presence as a leader had great influence in the minds of those affected and the general public and provided a connection that could not have otherwise been created. By being present, the leader sees for himself what is happening and, in the process, gets firsthand information from informal channels, has the opportunity to share his vision and communicate his perspective, and is able to forge a bond with stakeholders. At the same time, the stakeholders get access to the leader and are able to directly voice their concerns, ask questions about rumors, and make suggestions.[24] Hall took advantage of these opportunities to become intimately aware with the situation and determine what Ashland's response should be.

Hall held a press conference at 4:00 p.m., with what he later described as "half of Pittsburgh" in attendance. One summary of Hall's preparation for the press conference described it as a choice of "candor vs. liability." Hall clearly understood where Ashland Oil had failed, but he also knew that publicly admitting the errors could have serious legal ramifications, to include the loss of attorney-client privilege.[25] Harry Wiley, former director of advertising and communications for Ashland Oil, recalled, "I think the lawyers were calling the shots and the Communications Department was waiting to be told what to do."[26] As a principled leader focusing on realigning the situation and principles, Hall opted for candor. Wiley described what followed as "John Hall went up there and said 'it's our mistake, we did it, we'll fix it, we'll take care of it' and the lawyers went, 'Awww **.'"[27]

Hall demonstrated Craig Johnson's assertion that "responsibility is the foundation of ethical crisis leadership."[28] "On behalf of Ashland Oil," Hall told the press conference, "I want to apologize to the people of the Pittsburgh area." After Hall was done speaking, a member of the audience asked him if there was anything else he would like to add. Dan Lacy, former vice president of corporate affairs for Ashland Oil, recognized such a question as fraught with danger, but Hall did not back away from it. Lacy paraphrases Hall's response as, "Well at the end of the day, you always want to do what's right and that's just what we're trying to do." Lacy continues, "That was not a talking point. That was John under pressure; in the moment, speaking from the heart."[29] Such actions are consistent with Anna Simons's assessment that principled leaders "don't have to think about what *not* to do; they know from within."[30]

Overall, the spill and its aftermath cost Ashland an estimated $40 million, including $30 million to settle class-action civil lawsuits.[31] Still, Hall's expert handling of the crisis won high praise. Carnegie Mellon University named him "Crisis Manager of the Year," and the Harvard Business School uses him as a crisis management case study.[32] One of Stephen Covey's "means of influence" used by principle-centered leaders is to "admit your mistakes, apologize, ask for forgiveness." An apology does not make a violation of principles go away, but it does facilitate the realignment process. On the other hand, covering up, ignoring, or minimizing the violation serves to exacerbate the breach. Hall's handling of the Ashland Oil spill demonstrates how a principled leader's quick return to actions consistent with principles is the proper course.

Charles Spaulding and Cardinal Point No. 4

Principle: "There must be social service in business."[33]

Lesson: The discipline of thoughtfully and deliberately listing principles is fundamental to the practice of principled leadership.

From 1900 until his death in 1952, Charles Spaulding managed the North Carolina Mutual Life Insurance Company, America's largest Black-owned business. In large measure because of Spaulding and his business, Durham, North Carolina, became known as the "Black Wall Street." In 1937, Spaulding wrote an article for the *Southern Workman* titled "Business in Negro Durham." In the article, Spaulding identified four "cardinal points" that he deemed essential to running any business: character, fundamental business principles, cash or its equivalent, and social service in business. It was in his explanation of his fourth cardinal point that Spaulding established his principle that "there must be social service in business."[34]

Corporate social responsibility (CSR), as well as the related concepts of sustainability and environmental, social, and governance, have gained increasing visibility and traction over the past few decades. These practices all suggest that companies consider more than just financial factors in making business decisions. CSR specifically is "the idea that a company should be interested in and willing to help society and the environment as well as be concerned about the products and profits it makes."[35] Leon Prieto and Simone Phipps declare that "Spaulding may very well be one of the pioneers of CSR, both as a business thought leader and a practitioner."[36]

Spaulding grew up working hard on his father's farm in Columbus County, North Carolina. In 1894, he moved to Durham where he finished his schooling and did a number of odd jobs. His work ethic and enthusiasm soon attracted the attention of John Merrick and Aaron

Moore, the founders of Mutual Life Insurance Company. Merrick was a successful barber, and Moore was the only Black doctor in Durham. Their pursuit of these activities left them little time to manage Mutual, which by 1900 appeared to be on the brink of failure. To avoid that disaster, Merrick and Moore entrusted the 26-year-old Spaulding to reorganize the company.[37]

At this point in Durham, big insurance companies had little interest in insuring Blacks, who then often had to solicit funds from each other to bury one of their deceased. Spaulding immediately recognized the altruistic intention of Merrick and Moore to "end the humiliating practice which our people had to resort to at funerals." Because of this, Prieto and Phipps posit that Mutual always was a social enterprise that Spaulding would have to make not just financially successful but also successful, "as determined by the positive difference made in the lives of organizational members and the community at large."[38]

Mutual thrived under Spaulding's management. When he became general manager in 1900, he was literally the company's only employee. In 1904, he expanded Mutual's operation into South Carolina. In 1908, Mutual had 100,000 clients.[39] By 1916, he had extended the company's territory north from the Carolinas and Georgia into Virginia, Maryland, and Washington, D.C. By 1920, Mutual had a presence in almost every southern state, and in 1921, the company moved into a modern six-story building in Durham's largely white downtown. By 1924, Spaulding had added a fire insurance company, a savings and loan association, the Mortgage Company of Durham, and the National Negro Finance Association as sister institutions within the Mutual family. From near insolvency, Spaulding had built what became known as "The World's Largest Negro Business."[40]

In addition to this financial success, Spaulding managed Mutual to reflect his cardinal point that "there must be social service in business." "Cardinal" is a word not often used today in its adjective form, but it means "most important; having other things based on it."[41] Such a definition is compatible with William Safire's description of "principle" as meaning "a primary truth that formed the basis of other beliefs."[42] Indeed, Spaulding treated this cardinal point as a principle.

The cardinal point of social service informed Spaulding's

decisions on all levels. Mutual had been founded on the ideas of cooperation, thrift, diligence, and economic solidarity exemplified by Booker T. Washington. Under Spaulding, uplift of the Black race was codified as a salient feature of the company's culture.[43] When asked if operating Mutual might have been easier outside of the Jim Crow South, Spaulding replied that "ours was and is a business by and for Negroes, and it is here where Negroes live."[44] In pursuing this calling, Walter Weare describes Spaulding as a "New South broker for philanthropy and employment in black institutions."[45] Another observer noted that at Mutual, "the mere business aspect of the company was subordinated to a consideration of the economic salvation of the Negro race."[46]

Outside the company, Spaulding took many steps to help the Black community. Under his leadership, Mutual made funds available for projects such as Lincoln Hospital, North Carolina Central Hospital, a library, local churches, and three newspapers. He even shared business advice with his competitors such as in a 1927 article published in *The Messenger* magazine called "Dangerous Tendencies in Negro Business." Such efforts won Spaulding the nickname "Mr. Cooperation."[47]

Within the company, Spaulding endeavored to build in his employees "that good old Mutual spirit" that celebrated intrinsic reward independent of material reward. One aspect of this campaign was the "forum" which Spaulding began in 1921. This broad-reaching effort included a host of activities. Competitive spelling matches reflected the company's emphasis on education. Public speaking opportunities built confidence and oratory skills. Sessions to air grievances promoted civil society. Spaulding's insistence that employees from the lower ranks serve as leaders of the forum fostered growth and development. Outside speakers such as W.E.B. Du Bois and Eleanor Roosevelt exposed participants to the latest ideas. All of these components made self-improvement a central part of Spaulding's forum.[48]

Spaulding also provided social service to his employees by creating for them a workplace that met their personal needs. Within the Mutual building, employees could avail themselves of a modern clinic headed by a graduate of the Harvard Medical School, a printing press, and a cafeteria.[49] Women were welcome members of the Mutual workforce. Indeed in 1912, women comprised a majority, with 11 of the 20 full-time staff members being women. All of Spaulding's employees benefited from training programs designed to equip them with the tools needed to be successful and to prepare them for better paying jobs. Undergirding all these employee social service initiatives was Spaulding himself. He practiced a personal leadership style and was always available to his employees, leading most of them to refer to him as "Papa" in recognition of his role as a father figure within the Mutual family.[50]

Although Spaulding's social service centered on improving conditions for Blacks, he also worked to improve race relations in general, including serving as the secretary of the North Carolina Commission on Interracial Cooperation. As early as 1915, Spaulding was hiring white agents to work at Mutual, creating a safe work environment where Blacks and whites could cooperate and collaborate. "The trouble in America today," Spaulding wrote in 1940, "is a lack of understanding between the groups and races that compose this great nation of ours. The solution lies in a better understanding and a wholesome appreciation of the merits of each."[51] Commenting on this inclusiveness, Prieto and Phipps note that Spaulding "focused on a purpose-filled, development-oriented, rewarding mission that included his employees and their families, as well as his community (both black and white)."[52]

Spaulding's success as a Black businessman also allowed him to provide social services through political action. During the New Deal, Spaulding made recommendations to President Franklin D. Roosevelt regarding appointments to the "Black cabinet." As president of the Urban League's National Emergency Advisory Council, Spaulding became the official interpreter of the National Recovery Administration to the Black community. As chairman of the Durham Committee on Negro Affairs, Spaulding "charted the passage between two eras of southern politics and race relations, the passage between classic paternalism dating back to slavery and direct politics looking ahead to the civil rights movement." As a result, Black re-enfranchisement occurred in Durham some 20 years ahead of comparable southern cities. Weare notes that Spaulding was not just "the patriarch of black Durham" but that he also possessed "social and political influence extending throughout the southern region and beyond."[53]

Recall that the hypothesis for this research project was that "in order for there to be something called 'principled leadership,' there must be principles that serve as the focus of the leader's actions." Indeed, it seems intuitive that for "principled leadership" to be legitimate, at a minimum, the principles that inform it must be clearly stated and understood. CADRE's statement of "Beliefs, Values, and Principles" in Appendix 1 is offered as one example of an organization that has taken this prerequisite step. Spaulding's identification of his four cardinal points, to include his fourth one that "there must be social service in business" is another.

Recall also Safire's assertion that a principle is "a rule for ethical conduct."[54] If Safire is correct, the student of principled leadership must look deeper than Spaulding's overt behavior and find the underlying principle that inspired it. As a Black businessman, Spaulding believed in the principle that Mutual existed for reasons that transcended mere short-term economic gain. Because principles, Safire argues, form "the basis for other beliefs," this cardinal point led Spaulding to use Mutual and his own personal standing as a vehicle for a host of social service initiatives to help elevate the Black race.

Herb Kelleher and Leadership Philosophy

Principle: "Be yourself."[55]

Lesson: A philosophy of leadership informs the way a leader will use his principles to influence others.

George Ambler describes a leader's philosophy as "a set of beliefs, values, and principles that strongly influences how we interpret reality and guide our understanding of influencing humans."[56] Herb Kelleher served as chairman, president, and CEO of Southwest Airlines from 1981 to 2001. Under his leadership, Southwest was "the most consistently profitable, productive, and cost-efficient carrier in the industry."[57] His leadership philosophy is an excellent example of how beliefs, values, and principles shape a principled leader's actions.

The "beliefs" to which Ambler refers in his description of a leader's philosophy are the convictions people hold as true. They are derived from upbringing, culture, religious background, and traditions. One belief for Kelleher was that "business can and should be fun."[58] This belief helped Kelleher decide what sort of people to hire. His main criterion was attitude. "If you don't have a good attitude," he explained, "we don't want you, no matter how skilled you are. We can change skill levels through training. We can't change attitudes."[59] He also sought out employees who had personalities that separated them from the "humorless, self-centered, or complacent ... corporate clones" that filled the ranks of other airlines.[60] Harry Garner writes that "a well thought out leadership philosophy is a critical foundational tool to use to ... create positive organizational climates."[61] Once Kelleher had hired the right kind of people, he wanted to immerse them in a positive organizational climate that allowed them to have fun.

Under Kelleher, fun at Southwest took on many forms. In 1986, flight attendants began wearing shorts and tennis shoes, along with red polo shirts proclaiming that "Southwest Fliers Have More Fun." The mandatory safety briefings were sometimes given as a rap, and in-flight contests were held to see who had the largest holes in socks and stockings.[62] Kelleher even liked to get into the act himself. One Easter, he flew in a bunny costume, and once he showed up in the maintenance hangar at 2:00 a.m. dressed in drag as Klinger from the television show *M*A*S*H.* Kelleher saw fun as "a stimulant to people" and considered it to be beneficial to both employees and passengers. He believed employees who were having fun "enjoy their work more and work more productively." For his passengers, he wanted them to get off the plane thinking, "I didn't just get from A to B. I had one of the most pleasant experiences I have ever had and I'll be back for that reason."[63]

Values are deep-seated personal beliefs that shape a person's behavior. At Southwest, Kelleher was famous for valuing his employees. "You have to treat your employees like customers," he said. "When you treat them right, then they will treat your outside customers right.

That has been a powerful competitive weapon for us."[64] Because of this value, Kelleher led in a way "that nothing comes ahead of your people"[65] and believed that "the best leader is the best server."[66] Such servant leadership is one of the four value-based leadership theories Karen Hendrikz and Amos Engelbrecht integrated to develop their "construct" of principled leadership.[67]

Servant leadership is a leadership approach in which the leader meets the subordinate's legitimate needs.[68] In the uncertain airline industry, job security was a very important employee need. At one point, Kelleher was asked what his vision was for Southwest in the next 10 years. He got very serious and responded, "My vision is to keep Southwest Airlines job-secure for our people."[69]

When the Airline Deregulation Act removed federal control over such areas as fares, routes, and market entry of new airlines in 1978, few people foresaw the vulnerability it would create for employees in the industry.[70] In fact, the new exposure to competition led to heavy losses and conflicts with labor unions for a number of airlines. Not so with Southwest, where Kelleher noted, "we've never had layoffs. We could have made more money if we furloughed people. But we don't do that." Instead, Kelleher explained, "we honor [our employees] constantly. Our people know that if they are sick, we will take care of them. If there are occasions of grief or joy, we will be there with them. They know that we value them as people, not just cogs in a machine."[71] At Kelleher's memorial service in 2019, Gary Kelly, who became Southwest's CEO in 2004, said, "The philosophy, according to Herb, was put your people first, empower them, love them, respect them and take very, very good care of them, and then and only then can you deliver on your promise to serve your customers with really low cost."[72]

To lead by this delegation and empowerment, Kelleher inspired his workforce to identify with the company and to buy into the Southwest philosophy. Once this was accomplished, Kelleher said that control became unnecessary.[73] People knew what to do and did it. His job became not to issue orders but to learn about the problems people were having and to offer help.[74] The result was that people took responsibility for executing their duties without excessive supervision or coercion. Instead, they acted based on commitment. As an example, Kelleher notes that "because our low-fare strategy is so central to who we are, our employees are enormously cost-conscious." Based on this commitment to the Southwest business model, his managers rarely submitted inflated budget requests.[75]

Perhaps even more remarkably, when fuel costs soared in the wake of Iraq's 1990 invasion of Kuwait, nearly one-third of Southwest's 8,600 employees took voluntary pay deductions to help pay for fuel. Kelleher said this "Fuel from the Heart" program "indicated that the spirit of Southwest Airlines was alive."[76] It was an example of how employees "see Southwest as an ongoing institution," thinking years, instead of days, into the future.[77] Such outcomes are consistent with principled leadership's emphasis on building follower "commitment" rather than "compliance."[78]

Principles are moral rules or beliefs that help you know what is right and wrong and that influence your actions. They are fixed and absolute. Indeed, Kelleher wrote that in different situations you may "change your practices, but not your principles."[79] For him, the overriding principle at Southwest was that "you and your organization are true to yourselves."[80] Kelleher reminded himself that "you have to exercise a certain amount of judgment with respect to what you're capable of and what you're not."[81] This self-awareness helped Kelleher keep Southwest aligned with the high-frequency, short-distance, low-fare niche and model that made it successful. For his employees, Kelleher wanted them to come to work and be themselves, rather than "putting on a mask" so that they would "look different, talk different, act different" at work than they did elsewhere.[82] By allowing this individuality, Southwest became a fun place to work. In addition to servant leadership, this emphasis on authenticity is another important component of Hendrikz and Engelbrecht's "construct of principled leadership."[83]

Garner notes that "the way we see ourselves as leaders guides our actions, our behaviors, and our thoughts. It provides the foundation of how we influence others."[84] Kelleher's belief in having fun, the value he placed on his employees, and his principle of being yourself were essential to the way he saw himself and the way he led Southwest

Airlines and the organizational culture and climate he fostered. Kelleher demonstrates how a leadership philosophy not only articulates principles but also puts them into action.

Nonetheless, an illustrative disaster struck Southwest after the Kelleher era. In the midst of the 2022 Christmas travel peak, Southwest experienced a "massive meltdown" that resulted in more than 16,700 canceled flights and 2 million stranded passengers between December 20 and 29. The problem began in the wake of a large winter storm, but whereas other carriers recovered, Southwest's outdated technology and manual scheduling processes could not keep up with the rapid rate of changes wrought by cancellations and delays in the nation's flight system.[85] But of all the problems that conspired against Southwest, Beth Kowitt concluded that "a seeming breakdown of its famous 'people-first' culture needs to be on the top of that list."[86]

Indeed, critics were quick to malign Southwest's corporate leadership, particularly Kelleher's successor, Gary Kelly, for the decline that led to the disaster and the airline's poor response to it. Industry analyst Henry Harteveldt declared that Southwest's behavior "absolutely goes against everything Southwest culture stands for." Although one of the hallmarks of Southwest culture under Kelleher was "you've got to take the time to listen to people's ideas, in the years since his departure Southwest pilots and crew had been repeatedly warning of the risks posed by the airline's outdated technology."[87]

The saga of Southwest Airlines is a cautionary tale that if principles are indeed fixed and constant, they should transcend the ebb and flow of an organization's leadership and not be dependent on any one leader. If something was lost in the transition from Kelleher to Kelly, it is an example of the distinction James Collins makes between what he calls "Level 5" and "Level 4" leaders. According to Collins, Level 5 "great" leaders set up their successors for even greater success in the next generation. In contrast, with Level 4 "good" leaders, the organization's success is dependent on their own presence and declines after they depart.[88] Such would seem to be the case at Southwest.

Political Leaders

George Marshall and the Mission to China

Principle: If the president asks, do it.

Lesson: Principles help resolve moral dilemmas.

Principled leadership goes beyond value-based leadership to put values into action by adherence to principles. Among George Marshall's values were loyalty, duty, and service. After being the man that Winston Churchill called "the true organizer of victory" in World War II, one might think that Marshall had satisfactorily lived these values and was due a rest. Instead, new situations continued to present themselves in which the president of the United States requested Marshall's services. Maryann Glynn and Heather Jamerson argue that principled leadership "is not simply about having the right values or principles, but [is] also about being able to act on these principles when leaders find themselves in situations that may work against those principles and values."[1] Marshall's response to each new request for his loyalty, duty, and service exemplify this aspect of principled leadership.

During World War II, General Joseph Stillwell occupied several complicated and at times conflicting command roles. He was the U.S. chief of staff to Chiang Kai-shek, U.S. commander of the China-Burma-India theater, in general control of Lend-Lease aid to China, and acting deputy to Lord Louis Mountbatten in the Southeast Asia command. The pressures inherent to these immense responsibilities, the machinations of Chinese politics, and an irascible personality that earned him the nickname "Vinegar Joe" combined to make Stillwell's mission a difficult one. In August 1944, President Franklin Roosevelt appointed Major General Patrick Hurley as ambassador to

China in hopes that he could bring some calm to what had become a very tense situation.[2]

Instead, the difficulty between Stillwell and Chiang continued to worsen, and in October, Roosevelt concluded he had no choice but to recall Stillwell. Hurley was having his own difficulties, believing that Foreign Service personnel in China were undercutting his efforts and that Secretary of State James Byrnes was discounting his complaints. On November 27, 1945, an exasperated and angry Hurley announced his resignation while strongly criticizing the State Department and President Harry Truman's administration. Amid this turmoil, Secretary of Agriculture Clinton Anderson recommended Truman appoint General George Marshall to head a mission to China.[3]

Only days before on November 20, Truman had reluctantly accepted Marshall's resignation as chief of staff of the army. In a low-key ceremony on November 26, Marshall received the Distinguished Service Cross and said his farewells. The next day, he and his wife, Katherine, were to move to their home in Leesburg, Virginia, to settle into a new life together of rest and quiet. Instead, there was a phone call. Marshall answered it and heard Truman ask him to assume the role of special ambassador to China, with orders to leave immediately. Marshall did not relay the message to his wife, who, thinking nothing of the call, went upstairs for a nap. When she came down later, she heard on the radio the announcement of the news. Marshall explained that that had been the nature of the earlier call. "I could not bear to tell you," he explained, "until you had had your rest."[4]

Mrs. Marshall was understandably bitter that her husband had been called on to serve yet again.[5] Yet, for Marshall, refusing Truman's request was not an option. In 1920, Marshall had written Brigadier General John Mallory, then a professor at Virginia Military Institute, that one of the four things "essential ... to be[ing] a highly successful leader in war" was to "make a point of extreme loyalty, in thought and deed, to your chiefs' personally; and in your efforts to carry out their plans or policies, the less you approve the more energy you must direct to their accomplishment."[6] In that regard, Drew Middleton, who covered World War II and postwar Europe for the *New York Times*, likens Marshall to the Duke of Wellington, who, in response to being questioned about accepting a relatively minor position explained, "I am *nimmukwallah* as we say in the East; that is, I have ate of the King's salt and therefore, I conceive it to be my duty to serve with unhesitating zeal and cheerfulness, when or wherever the King or his government may think proper to employ me."[7]

Marshall's sacrifice certainly placed him on the moral high ground when those around him complained of their hardships. When Marshall called on Colonel James Davis to serve as a liaison with the War Department, Davis protested that he had spent nearly five years in the service and needed to return to his family and his law practice. Marshall wryly replied, "You know, Colonel, I had rather a difficult war too."[8] When Marshall arrived at the embassy in China, Chargé d'Affaires Walter Robertson told him he had already tried to resign twice and was presently using all the influence he had to return to his home and family. Robertson said, "And he looked at me, and he said, 'I want to go home too.' And he told me how at the end of six years as Chief of Staff, he had been asked to go to China." Then Marshall proceeded to talk about the mission at hand, leaving Robertson to lament, "and that's the way I happened to be in China until late 1946 after I had resigned in September 1945."[9]

On assuming the mission to China, Middleton observes that Marshall "had the cards stacked against him."[10] Mao Tse-tung had developed a credible Communist challenge to the Nationalist government of Chiang Kai-shek. The Kuomintang, or Chinese Nationalist Party, provided Chiang his base of power but also vociferously resisted any proposals of compromise with the Communists. While the Kuomintang selfishly clung to power with no intention of making a new system work, the Communists seemed to welcome the advantage they would gain by China's economic collapse, regardless of the long-term effects on the Chinese people.[11] Marshall found himself in what Forrest Pogue describes as a "thankless position involving a hopeless task."[12]

Against these long odds, in January 1946, Marshall was able to guide the Nationalists and the Communists to agree to a cease-fire in their civil war. The negotiations unraveled, however, as the two sides became irreconcilable in their political views for China's future. Marshall struggled on for the remainder of the year in a vain attempt to salvage the agreement, only to conclude that "it is now going to be necessary for the Chinese, themselves, to do the things I endeavored to lead them into." He was recalled to the United States in January 1947.

But the China mission would not be the end of Marshall's service to the nation. On his return to the United States until 1949, he was secretary of state. From 1949 to 1950, he headed the American Red Cross. From 1950 to 1951, he was secretary of defense. By then, his biographer says that Marshall accepted the post "as a duty his country had a right to expect."[13] Indeed, in each case, his principle to do his duty guided Marshall, regardless of the personal cost. Shortly after becoming secretary of defense, he told Anna Rosenberg, who would become his assistant secretary of defense for manpower, "there is a Mrs. Marshall and I promised her three times I would come home. And I haven't been able to do it."[14] Indeed, when Marshall first accepted the position, he planned to serve only six months. Then President Truman asked him to stay on until the end of June 1951 and then again until September 1. Forrest Pogue explains that "there was always a new crisis and no good time to go," so Marshall continued to serve.[15]

Pogue writes that Marshall accepted all of these difficult undertakings based on the same principle. He would do what the president asked him to do.[16] Adhering to that principle allowed Marshall to resolve what Rushworth Kidder calls an "ethical dilemma ... those right-versus-right situations where two core moral values come into conflict."[17] For Marshall, he had divided loyalties born of two conflicting duties. One was to give his wife the type of retirement they had planned for and which she well deserved. The other was to answer the call of his president and the needs of his country. In such dilemmas, "each side is firmly rooted in one of our basic, core values."[18] In Marshall's case, those core values were loyalty, duty, and service. Deciding which of the two "rights" in an ethical dilemma is the higher one and acting on that decision requires a moral courage "to elevate one or more key values above others."[19] Such moral courage, Kidder argues, is "driven by principle."[20] For Marshall, that principle was that he would do what the president asked him to do. That was the "higher right."

Carl Lutz and the Hungarian Jews

Principle: Protect the defenseless.
Lesson: Principled leaders influence others to emulate their behavior.

In January 1942, Carl Lutz was posted as vice consul of the Swiss legation in Budapest, Hungary, and became the head of the foreign interests division.[21] Lutz used his position to develop ingenious ways to protect the Jewish population in Budapest from genocide. It is difficult to accurately determine how many people Lutz saved, but a commonly cited figure is 62,000.[22] Beyond these personal contributions, Lutz set the example for other, often more well-known figures such as Raoul Wallenberg to initiate protective measures on behalf of the Jews. Leadership is about influencing others, and Lutz demonstrates how a principled leader can influence others to also take principled action.

Between 1938 and 1941, Hungary adopted three pieces of anti–Jewish legislation that were largely patterned after the Nuremberg laws of Nazi Germany and effectively excluded Jews from state and public office.[23] On November 20, 1940, under pressure from Germany, Prime Minister Pál Teleki signed the Tripartite Pact, aligning Hungary with the Axis powers of Germany, Italy, and Japan. When Lutz arrived in Budapest, Switzerland was one of five neutral states that had representation in the Hungarian capital. The others were the Holy See, Spain, Portugal, and Sweden. Switzerland and Sweden are of particular note because of the expanded responsibilities these two legations assumed. Switzerland represented the interests of a dozen countries, including the United States and Britain, that had severed diplomatic relations with Hungary. The Jewish Agency for Palestine also came to be under the Swiss legation's protection. Sweden represented Hungary's interests in Washington, London, and Berlin, as well as representing the Soviet Union's interests in Hungary. François Wisard notes that this situation allowed Sweden and Switzerland "to restrict or enlarge their field of action as appropriate to come to the aid of the persecuted Jews."[24]

In Budapest, Lutz had a staff of some 20 individuals. They quickly began issuing 300–400 protective passports (*Schutzpasse*) to Jewish and non–Jewish American and British citizens, and later 1,000 more to Yugoslav citizens. These actions inspired Sweden to establish protective passports for Jews with connections to Sweden.[25]

Lutz also participated in a very complex international operation involving British, Palestinian, Swedish, and Swiss participants that was set up in March 1942 to allow Jewish children living in Hungary to emigrate to Palestine. Lutz worked closely with Moshe Krausz, who ran the Budapest branch of the Jewish Agency for Palestine, to draw up lists of children and obtain the authorizations required for their safe departure and passage. By March 19, 1944, the day Germany invaded Hungary, Theo Tschuy estimates that thanks to these efforts, about 10,000 children had been able to leave Budapest for Palestine.[26]

Some 75,000 Jews lived within Hungary's borders, including those who had fled from Poland and Slovakia. Although persecution existed, Hungary was for many years the only area under Axis control or influence where Hitler's "final solution" had not been enacted. That changed in March 1944. With Soviet forces advancing and the Hungarian government seemingly poised to defect to the Allies, Hitler ordered an invasion of Hungary. Unable to devote the forces to a full-scale occupation, Hitler instead forced Hungary to appoint a government that would collaborate with the Nazis and to accept a contingent of supervisory officials. Among these was Adolf Eichmann who arrived with a commando squad to oversee the deportation of Hungary's Jews.[27]

Eichmann envisioned an operation lasting three months. First to be deported would be the Jews in Hungary's eastern, southeastern, and northern provinces that were closest to the advancing Soviet army. Last to be deported would be the Jews in the capital of Budapest. Eichmann got to work quickly. The first train left for Auschwitz-Birkenau on May 15, 1944, and within a matter of weeks, more than 430,000 Jews had been deported. Amid an international outcry, Miklós Horthy, head of Hungary's puppet government, called a halt to the deportations on July 6. By then, only the Jews in Budapest remained, and they were forced to mark themselves and the buildings in which they lived with yellow stars.[28]

At the time of the German occupation, thousands of Jews were in possession of certificates allowing them to enter Palestine. Although the Nazi authorities halted this legal emigration, in April, Lutz was able to gain exemption from forced labor for those holding certificates and give them shelter in his offices at the former U.S. legation on Szabadsag ter (Liberty Square). Lutz then entered negotiations, first with Edmund Veesenmayer, the German plenipotentiary in Hungary, and then with Eichmann, that granted Lutz the ability to issue 8,000 protective letters (*Schutzbriefe*) to those who had already been granted Palestine certificates.[29]

Paul Fabry, a member of the Hungarian resistance against the German occupation, describes Lutz as "always working, never stopping, going on, moving from one office to another, moving from one person to another, surrounded by desperate Jewish people ... [who] pestered him every day to do more.... The pressure was enormous."[30] One way that Lutz responded to this incredible urgency was to take great liberty with the *Schutzbriefe* authorization, creatively interpreting the agreement as applying to families rather than individuals. On this basis, Lutz reports authorizing not 8,000 but 50,000 protective letters.[31]

In July, Lutz persuaded the Hungarian puppet government to allow holders of protective letters to move into special safe houses run by the neutral countries that enjoyed diplomatic immunity. An "international ghetto" was formed that consisted of 122 safe houses. Switzerland was responsible for 76 houses that sheltered some 15,000 people.[32]

Working with Lutz at the Swiss legation offices were some 30 staff members of the Jewish Agency for Palestine. As more and more people thronged to Szabadsag ter in search of protective letters, the risk of reprisals from German or Hungarian officials increased. To relieve this pressure, Lutz annexed the empty show room of a nearby glass factory as the "Emigration Department of the Swiss Legation," and on July 24, the Jewish Agency staff moved into the "Glass House" where they enjoyed diplomatic immunity. The building also became a refuge for persecuted Jews, and by the end of October, some 800 people were living there. Lutz later rented two more buildings that housed an additional 4,000 people.[33]

The Jewish Agency staff were not the only individuals who worked with Lutz to safeguard Budapest's Jews. On July 9, "reinforcement arrived," writes Wisard, "in the form of Raoul Wallenberg" who became Sweden's special envoy in Budapest. Wallenberg quickly contacted Lutz to learn of his efforts, and Wallenberg too began issuing protective documents. He worked tirelessly on behalf of the Jews until he was captured by Soviet forces on January 17, 1945.[34] Wallenberg was part of what Simon Wiesenthal calls a "remarkable and mutually supportive team ... of which Consul Lutz was the leading figure."[35]

In 1964, Lutz was named "Righteous among the Nations," an honor bestowed on non–Jewish individuals for risking their lives to aid Jews during the Holocaust, by Yad Vashem, Israel's Holocaust memorial. Lutz is highlighted here not only for his individual actions as a principled leader but for "paving the way for [actions] of the other neutral countries."[36] In this role, Fabry says that

> Carl Lutz stood out like a monument because he was not only a human of great conscience and capacity, but he was also a Swiss patriot who was trying to prove that Switzerland stood for freedom, free expression, and free religion; that it had a liberal capacity to help people. He was an example of what can be done.[37]

Principled leaders not only act according to principles themselves; they influence others to do the same.

Abraham Lincoln and Emancipation

Principle: "The paramount object in [the U.S. Civil War] is to save the Union."[38]

Lesson: Even principled leaders must be pragmatic.

On September 22, 1862, President Abraham Lincoln issued an emancipation proclamation that was to go into effect on January 1, 1863. This announcement was the result of a gradual progression, and even it did not end slavery in the United States. The long, incremental approach taken by President Lincoln illustrates the tension between principles and pragmatics that seems to require the wisdom that the

Enlightenment philosopher Frances Hutcheson described as "the pursuing of the best ends by the best means."[39]

Construction on Fort Monroe, Virginia, began in 1819, and when it was completed, the massive structure off Hampton Roads served as the "Gibraltar of the Chesapeake." The fort was strong enough to remain in Federal hands even after Virginia seceded from the Union, and in May 1861, Lieutenant General Winfield Scott dispatched Major General Benjamin Butler to secure this strategic location. Butler arrived on May 22 and within days was presented with the need to decide how to handle slaves within Federal lines. On May 27, he initiated a policy in which he declared that slaves were "contraband," just like any property seized during time of war. Although Butler's action was contrary to official Federal policy, it continued informally until August when Congress enacted the First Confiscation Act. This law allowed Federal authorities to confiscate slaves used by Confederates for military purposes. Although the act was a small step on the long road toward emancipation, its purpose was focused more on harming the master than helping the slave. Its primary intent was to deprive the Confederacy of the military and economic benefit of slaves who were being used to erect fortifications, dig trenches, transport supplies, and other activities that aided the Confederate war effort. The law did not attempt to address any rights of the freed slaves or to even guarantee their freedom when the war ended.[40]

Another milestone occurred when Major General David Hunter issued an order after the capture of Fort Pulaski, Georgia, on April 11, 1862, that liberated all the slaves then in Federal hands. On May 9, Hunter issued another order freeing all the slaves in his Department of the South which included Georgia, Florida, and South Carolina. "The persons in these three States," proclaimed Hunter's General Order No. 11, "heretofore held as slaves, are … declared forever free." Such a move was too much, too fast for Lincoln, who at this point in the war advocated a more measured approach called "conciliation." This policy assumed that it was only a minority of slave-holding aristocratic fire-eaters that had misguidedly led the South into secession and that popular support for the Confederacy was lukewarm at best. If the Federals treated the Southerners mildly, they would soon return to their senses and the Union would be restored. On May 19, Lincoln nullified Hunter's orders on the grounds that the general had exceeded his authority.

Nonetheless, the Second Confiscation Act was passed in July 1862, which expanded the subject slaves from those being used to support the Confederacy to all slaves owned by a Confederate master. Owners who had taken a loyalty oath were allowed to keep their slaves. Again, the focus of the act was not primarily emancipation but rather weakening the Confederacy.[41]

Increasingly, however, Lincoln was realizing that the issue of slavery and the war were inseparable. Aside from any moral considerations, slave labor was sustaining the Confederate economy and even being used to construct military fortifications. Gradually, Lincoln moved away from the policy of conciliation, and on July 22, 1862, he showed his cabinet a preliminary draft of the Emancipation Proclamation. Secretary of State William Seward advised Lincoln that prematurely issuing the proclamation would appear desperate without an accompanying military victory. Lincoln agreed and waited for the battlefield victory that would give him an opportunity to make the proclamation public.[42]

This gradualism was unsatisfactory to Horace Greeley, the staunchly abolitionist editor of the *New York Tribune*. On August 20, 1862, he published a "Prayer for Twenty Millions" addressed to President Lincoln and expressing that Greeley and others were "sorely disappointed and deeply pained by the policy you seem to be pursuing with regard to the slaves of the Rebels." Greeley complained of the Confiscation Acts being "habitually disregarded" and of Lincoln's annulment of Hunter's and other emancipation initiatives. Decrying what he considered the half-hearted and incomplete efforts thus far, Greeley warned that "every hour of deference to Slavery is an hour of added and deepened peril to the Union." Refusing to sacrifice "Principle and Honor," the issue was very clear to Greeley.

Lincoln too was a man of principle and honor, but he had also to concern himself with pragmatics. Chief of these was that slavery was legal in Maryland, Kentucky, Missouri, and Delaware, but those states had remained loyal to the Union. Still there was strong pro–Confederate sentiment in several of them and Lincoln could ill-afford to alienate the border states. A hostile Maryland, for example, would leave the Federal capital surrounded.

On August 22, President Lincoln responded to his "old friend" Greeley, explaining his policy in a way "not meant to leave any one in doubt." For Lincoln, the "paramount object in this struggle *is* to save the Union, and is *not* either to save or to destroy slavery." He continued,

> If I could save the Union without freeing *any* slave I would do it, and if I could save it by freeing *all* the slaves I would do it; and if I could save it by freeing some and leaving others alone I would also do that. What I do about slavery, and the colored race, I do because I believe it helps to save the Union; and what I forbear, I forbear because I do *not* believe it would help to save the Union. I shall do *less* whenever I shall believe what I am doing hurts the cause, and I shall do *more* whenever I shall believe doing more will help the cause.[43]

Although the Battle of Antietam itself was a tactical draw, the fact that General Robert E. Lee was forced to order a withdrawal back to Virginia on September 18 made it a strategic victory for the Federals. That was enough to give President Lincoln the opportunity he had been waiting for to issue the Emancipation Proclamation. On September 22, Lincoln announced, "That on the first day of January, in the year of our Lord one thousand eight hundred and sixty-three, all persons held as slaves within any State or designated part of a State, the people whereof shall then be in rebellion against the United States, shall be then, thenceforward, and forever free."

Significantly, in the Emancipation Proclamation, Lincoln acted just as he had promised Greeley that he would. He had freed some of the slaves—those in the rebellious Confederacy—but not others—those in Maryland, Kentucky, Missouri, and Delaware that had remained in the Union. Slavery in the entire United States was not abolished until the Thirteenth Amendment was adopted in 1865.

Lincoln's approach to emancipation illustrates the tension between principles and pragmatics. Lincoln certainly understood it. He had concluded his response to Greeley with the note that "I have here stated my purpose according to my view of *official* duty; and I intend no modification of my oft-expressed *personal* wish that all men every where could be free."[44] In navigating an extremely difficult and complex situation, President Lincoln appears to have used principles in an aspirational sense that provided strategic direction in the midst of tactical pragmaticism. Whereas Greeley pressed the science of principled leadership, Lincoln demonstrated its art.

Mahatma Gandhi and Satyagraha

Principle: "Pursuit of truth [does] not admit of violence being inflicted on one's opponent but that he must be weaned from error by patience and sympathy ... and patience means self-suffering."[45]

Lesson: Precommit to follow your principles.

Mahatma Gandhi is most famous for his campaign for India's independence from British rule, but before that, he was an advocate for Indian rights in South Africa. It was in South Africa that Gandhi first developed his strategy and tactics of nonviolence that were represented by satyagraha or "truth force." Gandhi explained that the "pursuit of truth [does] not admit of violence being inflicted on one's opponent but that he must be weaned from error by patience and sympathy." He added that "patience means self-suffering."[46] Thus, when Gandhi's peaceful protests were met by brutal governmental responses, such as what occurred during the Salt March of 1930, Gandhi's precommitment to the principle of satyagraha directed him to not respond to violence with violence, regardless of the personal costs. Gandhi's decision to reject violence represents the step in the principled leadership process that requires the elimination of all solutions that are inconsistent with the principles.

Economist Thomas Schelling discovered that he and many others "spend a good part of our time trying to get ourselves to do what we already decided to do."[47] He then went on to describe several "little tricks" such as not carrying cigarettes if you are trying to quit smoking that "we play on ourselves to make us do the things we ought to do or to keep us from the things we ought to foreswear."[48] To reduce the cognitive dissonance between the desires of our old self and the actions of our future selves, Schelling suggested "precommitting" as a paradoxical means of a person improving their chances of success by limiting their options.

When applied to principled leadership, Schelling's idea of precommitment removes from the decision-maker the temptation to select a momentarily pleasing alternative that violates deep standing principles. It facilitates the discipline required to subordinate impulses to values.[49] By precommitting to practice behaviors that were consistent with his principle of satyagraha and disqualify those that were not, Gandhi guarded against the weakness born of rationalization and opportunism.

Gandhi was born in India in 1869 but moved to London in 1888 to pursue studies in English and law. In 1893, he was contacted by Dada Abdullah, owner of a large shipping business in South Africa, on behalf of his cousin in Johannesburg who needed a lawyer. Gandhi accepted the position and, at age 23, set sail for South Africa. He would go on to spend 21 years there, and it was in South Africa that he developed much of the frame of reference, to include the commitment to satyagraha, that would inform much of his life's work.[50]

One of the conditions of the Pretoria Convention of 1881 which ended the First Boer War was that the Transvaal—the territory between the Vaal River in the south and the Limpopo River in the north—would be subject to British suzerainty. The British used this authority to impose a series of repressive indignities and injustices on the Indians living in there. Among these measures were the requirement to pay a poll tax to enter the region, the inability to own land except in areas set apart for them, no franchise, prohibition from walking on public footpaths, and not being able to be outdoors without a permit after 9:00 p.m.[51]

Conditions worsened in August 1906 with the passage of the Transvaal Asiatic Law Amendment Ordinance. The ordinance required every Asiatic (of which Indians were counted) over eight years of age to register before the Registrar of Asiatics. Indians had to have their finger- and thumbprints taken to obtain a registration permit and to produce those permits on request. Failure to register was a deportable offense. Gandhi recalled that "I shuddered as I read the sections of the Ordinance one after another. I saw nothing in it except hatred of Indians."[52]

On September 11, more than 3,000 Indians and Chinese gathered in the Empire Theatre in Johannesburg to protest the Transvaal Asiatic Law Amendment Ordinance. During the course of the meeting, Gandhi explained the greater magnitude of an oath made in the name of God as opposed to an ordinary resolution. Understanding this distinction, the assembly resolved to oppose the ordinance, if it became law, in the name of God. Resolution 4 declared that "British Indians here assembled solemnly and regretfully resolve that, rather than submit to the galling, tyrannous, and un–British requirements laid down in the above Draft Ordinance, every British Indian in the Transvaal shall submit himself to imprisonment and shall continue to do so until it shall please His Most Gracious Majesty the King-Emperor to grant relief."[53] This pledge became known as the "satyagraha oath."

Gandhi notes, however, that "the principle called *satyagraha* came into being before that name was invented." Before that, the English expression "passive resistance" was often used to describe the struggle, and Gandhi found that Europeans construed that term very narrowly and that "it was supposed to be a weapon of the weak, that it could be characterized by hatred, and that it could finally manifest itself as violence." Gandhi offered a nominal prize through *India Opinion*, a weekly newspaper he had founded in 1903, to the reader who could suggest the best name for the struggle, and from that was born "satyagraha."[54]

The Transvaal Asiatic Law Amendment Ordinance became law on May 9, 1907, and 155 Indians were imprisoned for refusing to register in January 1908. Between then and May 1908, Gandhi was imprisoned three times for a total of six months. He was imprisoned again from October to December. Throughout the campaign, some 3,000 people were arrested, 85 were deported, and 6,000 Indians left the province. In the end, the campaign failed to reverse the oppression and secure the general rights of Indian citizens. What the campaign did achieve, though, was to mark a shift in tactics from a purely constitutional approach toward one focused on the active participation of masses of ordinary people.[55] Perhaps more importantly, it marked "the birth of *satyagraha*,"[56] of which Gandhi writes that "the history of this struggle is for all practical purposes a history of the remainder of my life in South Africa and especially of my experiments with truth in that subcontinent."[57]

Gandhi was armed with these experiences when he returned to India in 1915. In 1921, he assumed leadership of the Indian National Congress. On January 26, 1930, the congress officially promulgated its declaration of independence from Britain, a declaration that the British rejected. In the wake of this development, Gandhi chose a campaign against the British salt tax as "the centerpiece of a new countrywide movement against the colonial government."[58] It was, claims Gandhi's biographer Ramachandra Guha, a decision that "was very likely influenced by the last of [Gandhi's] *satyagrahas* in South Africa."[59]

The salt marsh satyagraha began with Gandhi writing a letter to Lord Irwin, the viceroy of India, on March 2, 1930, declaring the salt tax to be "a curse" that "has impoverished the dumb millions by a system of progressive exploitation and by a ruinously expensive military and civil administration.... It has reduced us politically to serfdom." Gandhi also emphasized that in spite of this oppression, he remained committed to an "unquestionable and immovable faith in the efficacy of non-violence." He understood that some would consider his confidence in nonviolence to be a "mad risk," but Gandhi found strength in the knowledge that "the victories of truth have never been won without risks, often of the greatest character."[60]

The salt tax protest took the form of a 241-mile march from Ahmedabad to Dandi, which Gandhi begun on March 12 with 78 volunteers. Gandhi made several speeches to throngs of people along the way, and thousands of protesters joined him when he reached Dandi on April 5. The next morning, he rose before dawn and led a group of marchers to the sea where he defied the law by picking up a few lumps of natural salt lying in a small pit.[61] Inspired by Gandhi's action in Dandi, similar breaches of the law were occurring throughout India, and Gandhi went from village to village, encouraging people to break the salt law and invite arrest.[62] On May 4, Gandhi drafted a letter to

Irwin, announcing his intention to lead a raid on the Dharasana Salt Works, but before Gandhi could post the letter or execute his plan, he was arrested on May 5.[63]

Nonetheless, Gandhi's followers went ahead with the protest without him on May 21. In doing so, they experienced those "risks ... of the greatest character" that Gandhi had alluded to, but in keeping with the principle of satyagraha, they offered no resistance. American journalist Webb Miller described the scene:

> Suddenly, at a word of command, scores of native policemen rushed upon the advancing marchers and rained blows on their heads with their steel-shot lathis [long bamboo sticks]. Not one of the marchers even raised an arm to fend off blows. They went down like ten-pins. From where I stood I heard the sickening whack of the clubs on unprotected skulls.... In two or three minutes the ground was quilted with bodies.... The survivors without breaking ranks silently and doggedly marched on until struck down.... Group after group walked forward, sat down, and submitted to being beaten into insensibility without raising an arm to fend off the blows.[64]

The brutality went on for hours, leaving many seriously injured and two killed.

Reports such as Miller's were published worldwide, drawing much attention and support for Gandhi and his cause. With Gandhi in jail, *Time* magazine reported that "not thousands but millions of Indians are taking individual beatings which they could escape by paying what His Majesty's Government calls, quite accurately, 'normal taxes.'" The magazine went on to name Gandhi its Man of the Year for 1930.[65]

The powerful impact of the salt march satyagraha caught the British off guard, and on January 26, 1931, they released Gandhi from prison. Desperate to end the salt tax boycott, Irwin offered to enter into talks with Gandhi. While the resulting Gandhi-Irwin pact was incomplete from the Indian perspective, it did resolve that in exchange for an end to the boycott, all the prisoners taken during the protests would be released, residents of coastal areas would be allowed to make their own salt, and nonaggressive picketing of shops selling alcohol or foreign cloth would be permitted. Perhaps more important for the future, Talat Ahmed notes that, as a result of the exchange, "a respect and even fondness had developed between Irwin and Gandhi" and that Gandhi was now "talking to the viceroy as an equal for the first time on behalf of India."[66]

Much work remained to be done until India finally achieved independence in 1947. Gandhi would be arrested and jailed from January 1932 to May 1933, in August 1933, and from August 1942 to May 1944.[67] All told, it is estimated that Gandhi spent a total of 2,338 days in jail in South Africa and India. Through it all, he held steadfastly to the principle of satyagraha, which will be recalled, means "truth force." Gandhi concludes his autobiography stating that "to see the universal and all-pervading Spirit of Truth face to face one must be able to love the meanest of creation as oneself."[68] For Gandhi, that truth and that love "did not admit of violence being inflicted on one's opponent but that he must be weaned from error by patience and sympathy."[69] Gandhi precommitted to this principle when he took the "satyagraha oath" in 1906 in South Africa. Having done so, it sustained him until his work was finished.

Military Leaders

John McCain and Being a Prisoner of War

Principle: "I will accept neither parole nor special favors from the enemy."[1]

Lesson: Organizations build alignment through training.

Over 3,600 American servicemen were held as POWs during the Korean War. Many were subjected to inhumane treatment, beatings, threats, and "brainwashing" in an unprecedented effort by their Communist captors to manipulate and exploit the POWs as part of an international propaganda campaign. Under such conditions, many prisoners collaborated with the enemy. At the time of the armistice, 21 Americans even refused repatriation and opted to remain with the Communists in Korea. Such behavior was a deviation from what was expected of the American serviceman, and after reflecting on what caused this situation, the Department of Defense embarked on a training program to restore principled behavior. As a POW in the Vietnam War, John McCain drew on this training.

Colonel Franklin Brooke Nihart commanded the Second Battalion, First Marine Regiment, First Marine Division in the Korean War and earned the Navy Cross for his actions at the Battle of the Punchbowl. After the war, he served on the Department of Defense's Advisory Committee on Prisoners of War. The committee concluded that many of the American POWs who had collaborated with the enemy were unprepared for and ill-equipped to deal with the type of treatment imposed on them by the Communists. Nihart set out to write a code of conduct to serve as guidelines for future POWs. On August 17, 1955, President Dwight Eisenhower signed Executive Order 10631—Code of Conduct for Members of the Armed Forces of the United

States. The order states that "all members of the Armed Forces of the United States are expected to measure up to the standards embodied in this Code of Conduct while in combat or in captivity."[2]

The code has been amended on three occasions for small purposes such as to make it gender neutral, but in its original form, it stated:

I. I am an American fighting man. I serve in the forces which guard my country and our way of life. I am prepared to give my life in their defense.

II. I will never surrender of my own free will. If in command, I will never surrender my men while they still have the means to resist.

III. If I am captured, I will continue to resist by all means available. I will make every effort to escape and aid others to escape. I will accept neither parole nor special favors from the enemy.

IV. If I become a prisoner of war, I will keep faith with my fellow prisoners. I will give no information, or take part in any action which might be harmful to my comrades. If I am senior, I will take command. If not, I will obey the lawful orders of those appointed over me and will back them up in every way.

V. When questioned, should I become a prisoner of war, I am bound to give only name, rank, service number and date of birth. I will evade answering further questions to the utmost of my ability. I will make no oral or written statements disloyal to my country and its allies or harmful to their cause.

VI. I will never forget that I am an American fighting man, responsible for my actions, and dedicated to the principles which made my country free. I will trust in my God and in the United States of America.[3]

On October 26, 1967, Lieutenant Commander John McCain III was flying a bombing mission over Hanoi, North Vietnam, when his Douglas A-4 Skyhawk was hit by a Russian surface-to-air missile. McCain was able to eject from the aircraft but suffered broken bones in both arms and his right leg. He landed in a lake and was quickly captured by local North Vietnamese. He was stripped of his clothes, struck on the shoulder with a rifle butt, and bayonetted in his ankle and groin before being taken to Hanoi's main prison. There, he was accused of war crimes, interrogated, and beaten. He was told, "You will not receive any medical treatment until you talk." Only when the North Vietnamese realized that McCain's father was a navy admiral, at that time stationed in London as the commander in chief, U.S. naval forces, Europe, did they give McCain some semblance of medical care. The Communists quickly began exploiting McCain's capture for propaganda purposes, declaring, "We have the crown prince."

In December, McCain was transferred to another compound in Hanoi that the POWs called "The Plantation." He was subject to regular interrogation and poor treatment, but McCain reports, "they were not torturing me at this time," and he was refusing to cooperate. Then in June 1968, an interrogator McCain calls "the Cat," who was the commander of all the prison camps, abruptly asked him if he wanted to go home. At this time, McCain was severely malnourished and underweight after having suffered from dysentery for about a year and a half. He "was worried whether I could stay alive or not." Moreover, he did not have any communication with the camp's senior American officer, and he would have to decide what to do without any advice. The Cat gave McCain three days to think about it. As he did, McCain remembered Article III of the Code of Conduct which specified, "I will accept neither parole nor special favors from the enemy." McCain concluded that going home before other prisoners who had been there longer would be accepting special favors.

When the Cat asked McCain for his decision, McCain told him "no." The Cat demanded to know why, and McCain told him that "American prisoners cannot accept parole, or amnesty or special favors. We must be released in the order of our capture." The Cat tried other tactics, including telling McCain that President Lyndon Johnson had ordered him to go home and showing McCain a letter from his wife saying, "I wished that you had been one of those three who got to come home." The Cat also claimed that the doctors had told him that McCain would not survive unless he received medical treatment in the United States. Still, McCain refused. Three nights later, the Cat repeated his tactics with the same result. Then on the morning of July 4, the day McCain's father was to assume command of Pacific Command in Hawai'i, McCain was called to appear before the Cat and another interrogator McCain calls "the Rabbit." McCain later surmised the North Vietnamese wanted to coincide his release with his father's assumption of command so they could advertise it as a humane gesture and also use it to exploit class consciousness in the United States. McCain imagined them saying, "Look, you poor devils, the son of the man who is running the war has gone home and left you here. No one cares about you ordinary fellows." McCain "determined at all times to prevent any exploitation of my father and my family."

The Rabbit demanded, "Our senior wants to know your final answer." McCain told him, "My final answer is the same. It's 'No.'" The Cat exploded, breaking his pen in two and kicking over a chair. "They taught you too well. They taught you too well," he exclaimed as he stormed out of the room and slammed the door.[4] "Yes," McCain wrote later, "they had."[5]

Indeed, McCain had been taught well. Executive Order 10631 did not just enumerate the articles of the Code of Conduct. It also specified that "to ensure achievement of these standards, members of the armed forces liable to capture shall be provided with specific training and instruction designed to better equip them to counter and withstand all enemy efforts against them, and shall be fully instructed as to the behavior and obligations expected of them during combat or captivity."[6] In "The US Fighting Man's Code," the Office of Armed Forces Information and Education expanded on this requirement by articulating "instructional material" for each article. For Article III, this material explained that "parole agreements are promises given the captor by a prisoner of war upon his faith and honor, to fulfill stated conditions, such as not to bear arms or not to escape, in consideration of special privileges, usually release from captivity or lessened restraint. He will never sign or enter into a parole agreement."[7] McCain drew on this principle and this training to refuse what he considered to be the special privilege of early release.

After the Cat left, the Rabbit said, "Now, McCain, it will be very bad for you," and that proved to be true. McCain matter-of-factly reports, "I was set up for some very severe treatment which lasted for the next year and a half."[8] After nearly five and a half years of captivity, McCain was released on March 14, 1973, as part of Operation Homecoming. He was among 107 other aviators who had been shot down in 1967 and 1968 (there was one exception who had been shot down in December 1971).[9] Other than prisoners who were seriously injured, the order of release was based on length of captivity.

In addition to its amazing testimony to one man's endurance and courage, John McCain's story illustrates some of an organization's responsibilities in building a culture of principled leadership. As the military studied the experience of American prisoners during the Korean War, it discovered that expected and actual behavior were out of alignment. The military decided that a code of conduct was necessary to help its members uphold their values in captivity. But rather than just creating a list, the military developed a training program to ensure practical alignment. Even the Cat recognized that it was McCain's training that allowed him to stand by his principles.

Katumba Wamala and Trust

Principle: "There is nothing as important as peace."

Lesson: The consistency of principled leadership helps build trust.

Principled leadership is a very consistent form of leadership because the leader's actions are based on impersonal, factual, objective, and self-evident principles.[10] Many other forms of leadership are much more subjective. Charismatic leadership is subject to the personality of the leader. Transactional leadership is subject to the continued ability of the leader to negotiate an acceptable arrangement. Leader-member exchange leadership is subject to the relationship between the leader and the led. While principled leadership empowers the leader to use creativity and imagination to solve leadership challenges, all the solutions must be consistent with the principles. This consistency builds trust between leader and the led, even in situations otherwise marked by ambiguity, change, and uncertainty. As the chief of the Ugandan People's Defense Forces (UPDF) during the run-up to the 2016 Ugandan presidential and parliamentary election, General Katumba Wamala found himself in such a fluid environment, but his principled leadership built trust between himself and others.

Ryan Gibb describes presidential politics in Uganda as "a national drama," and the February 18, 2016, elections for president, the national assembly, and local councils certainly reinforced this assessment. Uganda had reintroduced a multiparty system in 2004, but the National Resistance Movement (NRM), which boasted the incumbent president and control of parliament, had a long history of using intimidation and harassment of opposition candidates to create what Gibb describes as a "lopsided political arena."[11]

Campaigning began on November 9, 2015, with the most competitive presidential contenders being incumbent Yoweri Museveni of the NRM, Kizza Besigye of the Forum for Democratic Change (FDC), and Amama Mbabazi of the newly formed Go Forward Party. The NRM was the clear front-runner. Counting his term during Uganda's period as a one-party state, President Museveni had been in power for four terms. He spent roughly $7 million on the campaign, about 12 times as much as Besigye and Mbabazi's combined amount.

Nonetheless, the NRM had been plagued by infighting, and Mbabazi in particular posed a unique challenge to Museveni. As the former NRM prime minister, Mbabazi drew support from the party base. To stave off these threats, Museveni and the NRM took decisive and provocative action to protect their dominant position.

It is not uncommon for many authoritarian governments to use the police more to secure the regime than to protect and serve the citizenry. Specifically in Uganda, the International Crisis Group notes that Museveni "controls key institutions, including the army and police that guarantee his political survival."[12] In their analysis of the 2016 Ugandan elections, Sam Wilkins and Richard Vokes describe an "electoral machine" wielded by Museveni that includes "the use of coercion and intimidation by state security forces and their various militia."[13]

One such measure was the recruitment of as many as 2.5 million "crime preventers" to act as Museveni's vanguard. Ostensibly intended to protect villages during the elections, these extra-constitutional constables were instead determined by Amnesty International, Human Rights Watch, Human Rights Network Uganda, Chapter Four Uganda, and the Human Rights Initiative to have "acted in partisan ways and have carried out brutal assaults and extortion with no accountability." The NRM government also blocked Twitter and SMS services, claiming that the public would use these social media platforms to incite violence. On July 9, 2015, the government went so far as to place Go Forward's Mbabazi and FDC's Besigye under "preventative arrest."[14] On January 24, 2016, NRM secretary general Justine Lumumba warned that the state would shoot to kill anyone who protested the election results. A week later, Assistant Resident District Commissioner of Jinja Eric Sakwa issued a similar statement.[15]

It was this situation that Wamala faced as chief of the UPDF. Fortunately, Wamala had had several previous experiences that had helped him be well prepared for the challenge. His career began in 1980 as an officer in the Uganda National Liberation Army (UNLA), which had become the national army after the overthrow of Idi Amin in 1979. In 1986, the UNLA was defeated by Museveni's National Resistance Army (NRA), and Wamala transitioned into the NRA.

From 1999 to 2000, Wamala was a student at the U.S. Army War College in Carlisle, Pennsylvania. After graduation, Wamala was promoted to major general and commanded UPDF forces in the Democratic Republic of the Congo until 2001. He next participated in "Operation Iron Fist," a UPDF offensive against Lord's Resistance Army bases in southern Sudan. Wamala was then appointed inspector general of police, a post he held until 2005. Promoted to lieutenant general, Wamala became commander of Uganda's Land Forces. In this capacity, he was active in the African Union Mission in Somalia (AMISOM), a regional peacekeeping mission operated by the African Union with the approval of the United Nations. In 2013, Wamala was promoted to four-star general and appointed chief of Uganda's Defense Forces. His career of distinguished service was well recognized by the U.S. military. In 2014, he was inducted into the U.S. Army War College's International Hall of Fame, and in 2015, he and five colleagues became the first Ugandans to be awarded the U.S. Army's Legion of Merit.[16] His proven record of service led him to be "regarded as one of Uganda's most respected politicians and military men."[17]

As Wamala surveyed the current situation, he was already intimately familiar with the political machinery in Uganda. He had lived through the abusive regime of Idi Amin, and he had made the transition when Museveni came to power. He had gleaned valuable leadership experience commanding at the highest levels and leading large-scale military operations. His experience with the police had familiarized him with law enforcement and the difference between police and military roles and missions. His service with AMISOM had been dedicated to keeping the peace. Perhaps most significantly, his experience at the U.S. Army War College and his operational cooperation with the U.S. military had exposed him to the American military's institutional professionalism and values.

Determined to calm fears, at the start of the campaign in 2015, Wamala told the UPDF that "all army officers are cautioned not to dare engage in politics and anybody who breaks the law will be dealt with." He added later that the army's role "was not shooting civilians, but preserving the peace and enabling people to exercise their right to choose." Drawing on his experience with the U.S. Army, on February 6, 2016, he reassured an anxious public by noting that "the motto of the army war college I went to was 'not to promote war but to preserve peace.'"[18]

Paul Nantulya explains that "Wamala's record of service as a respected officer and reputation for having zero tolerance for political meddling lent credibility to his appeals. His statements on the eve of the polls were therefore viewed as consistent and trustworthy." Nantulya concludes that Wamala's timely messaging "helped defuse public anxiety and reinforced respect for the military's nonpartisanship."[19]

In the end, Musevini was elected for a fifth term as president with 61 percent of the vote, and the NRM won 199 of the 289 seats in the general parliamentary election. A host of international observers, including U.S. secretary of state John Kerry, questioned the credibility and transparency of the election, and Besigye, who finished second in the polling, was placed under house arrest by police who claimed he planned to announce "purportedly final results" that would have amounted to "disturbing public order."[20] Nonetheless, the postelection period turned out to be "relatively calm," an outcome Nantulya credits to Wamala and his example of "how ethical leadership is central to maintaining public trust in the security sector and ultimately preserving stability and peace."[21]

James Kouzes and Barry Posner write that "the very first step on the journey to credible leadership is clarifying your values—discovering those fundamental beliefs that will guide your decisions and actions."[22] For Wamala, this discovery was informed in large part by his participation in peacekeeping operations like AMISOM and by his experience at the Army War College. From its motto, Wamala concluded "there is nothing as important as peace."[23] When confronted with the prospect of election violence, Wamala drew clarity from this principle, and his consistency in following it won him the trust of those around him.

John Boyd and Careerism

Principle: You must choose to either be someone or do something.

Lesson: Principled leadership requires commitment to something bigger than yourself.

Air force colonel John Boyd's biographer Robert Coram calls Boyd "that rarest of creatures—a *thinking* fighter pilot." Boyd's intellect led him to develop the energy-maneuverability (E-M) theory, which stressed that maneuverability was more important than speed and influenced the air force to adopt the F-15 Eagle as its air superiority fighter in 1967. But Boyd's staunch advocacy of his theory often placed him at odds with the air force bureaucracy, to the detriment, he felt, of his career advancement. Nonetheless, for Boyd, the choice "to either be someone or do something" was clear.

In 1973, Boyd explained his principle to Raymond Leopold, an air force captain newly assigned to the Pentagon. "Tiger," Boyd told Leopold, "one day you will come to a fork in the road. And you're going to have to make a decision about which direction you want to go. If you go that way, you can be somebody. You will have to make compromises and you will have to turn your back on your friends. But you will be a member of the club and you will get promoted and you will get good assignments." The other path was one that Boyd depicted as being costlier but more rewarding. If Leopold were to choose it, Boyd foretold, "you can do something—something for your country and for your Air Force and for yourself. If you decide you want to do something, you may not get promoted and you may not get the good assignments and you certainly will not be a favorite."[24] Boyd's perspective is a reminder that the steadfast pursuit of principles may be isolating and lonely.

Boyd enlisted in the Army Air Corps in 1944 while still a junior in high school. He served briefly as a mechanic for aircraft turrets at Lowry Field, Colorado, before going to Japan as part of the occupation force. He was discharged in 1947.

Back in the United States, Boyd enrolled in the University of Iowa. He took ROTC, and when he graduated in 1951, he was commissioned in the air force. After training in Albuquerque, New Mexico, and Columbus, Mississippi, Boyd served as an F-86 pilot in Korea. After the war, he attended the prestigious Fighter Weapons School at Nellis Air Force Base, Nevada, and did well enough to be assigned there as an instructor after graduation. Boyd rose to head the Academic Section and wrote the *Aerial Attack Study*, a manual for fighter tactics that explored "the science of fighter-versus-fighter combat" and "the geometric space relationships" the fighter pilot must understand.[25] After this assignment, Boyd attended Georgia Tech where he studied engineering, particularly the relationships between energy and energy changes of aircraft in flight. While there, Boyd devised a method to measure aircraft maneuverability, which is the ability to change altitude, airspeed, and direction.[26] He graduated in 1962, was promoted to major, and assigned to Eglin Air Force Base, Florida.[27]

At Eglin, Boyd met Thomas Christie, a mathematician who saw promise in Boyd's work and helped him gain access to a large-capacity, high-speed computer to confirm his calculations. Boyd ultimately codified his research as the E-M theory, which "allowed, for the first time, the calculation of an aircraft's performance based on its design characteristics; or, conversely, one could calculate the optimum aircraft design required to deliver a desired performance." As Boyd compared performance data between American and Soviet equivalent aircraft, he found that in most performance categories, the Soviet planes were superior.[28]

Boyd then began briefing his findings in what Ian Brown describes as a campaign of "pushing rightness on others." In the process, Brown reports that "generals and engineers alike cursed [Boyd], berated him, and even threatened him with a court-martial for stealing government resources to work on this entirely unsanctioned project."[29] Jacob Neufeld credits Brigadier General Allman Culberston, Air Proving Ground Center vice commander, with helping Boyd and Christie "fight off repeated attempts to terminate their studies,"[30] but Brown notes that the reason that Boyd "came through unscathed [was] because the data provided by his theory proved indisputably correct."[31]

In the end, Boyd made his case and, in so doing, was able to give the United States the ability to correct its deficiency before the Soviets even knew it existed. For this valuable contribution, Boyd received two air force scientific awards, and in October 1966, he was reassigned to the Pentagon to help fix problems found in the F-X project, the air force's latest fighter design. He was promoted to lieutenant colonel in 1967.[32]

Still, the debate continued in the lower levels of the American fighter community about whether the sophisticated high-tech American avionics systems were worth the added weight and reduced maneuverability. Based on his work with the E-M theory, Boyd championed sacrificing avionics for performance. While working on the F-X project, he found common cause with Pierre Sprey, a weapons system analyst in the Office of the Assistant Secretary of Defense, Systems Analysis, and the pair began advocating for a clear weather, air-to-air combat fighter with a reduced top speed but lighter weight and better performance. Much of the air force conventional wisdom, however, resisted Boyd's concept because of its shorter range and limited load-carrying capability. Boyd also suffered from a lack of credibility because he was not actively flying. After Boyd delivered a poorly received briefing to the TOPGUN instructors at the Navy Fighter Weapons School in Miramar, California, Commander Ron "Mugs" McKeown said, "Never trust anyone who would rather kick your ass with a slide rule than with a jet."[33] Undeterred, Boyd and Sprey grandly christened themselves as the "Reformers" and persisted with their "out of the box" thinking, ultimately developing what would become the McDonnel Douglas F-15 Eagle.[34]

Boyd's next assignment took him to Andrews Air Force Base, Maryland, in October 1969, to take the F-15 from concept to reality. Because he felt that last-minute design changes had deprived the F-15 of its E-M-derived performance purity, Boyd lost some enthusiasm about seeing the project come to fruition.[35] In 1971, he was promoted to colonel, and in 1972, he was posted to Thailand as vice commander of Task Force Alpha, an organization responsible for monitoring the sensor system along the Ho Chi Minh Trail where it passed through Laos. He returned to the Pentagon in May 1973 as director of Operational Requirements and Development Plans.

Boyd found his official work in his new job unfulfilling and turned much of his attention to using E-M theory to help guide development of what would become the F-16. Brown says that Boyd did this work "in the face of constant conflict with both individual and institutional resistance to change" and found the air force and Department of Defense to be "uninterested in opening their collective minds and learning new things." By 1975, Brown concludes, "Boyd had evidently tired of being one of the few men who wanted 'to do' in a bureaucracy run by those who preferred 'to be.'" In August, Boyd retired from active duty.[36] When he died in 1997, he was, according to Robert Coram, "one of the most important unknown men of his time."[37]

A word of caution is probably in order as we consider Boyd as a case study of principled leadership. Marshall Michel describes Boyd as "glib, iconoclastic, ambitious, self-aggrandizing" and more "critic" than "reformer."[38] Coram notes that "while in his professional life Boyd accomplished things that can never be duplicated, in his personal life he did things few would want to duplicate."[39] In the search for an exemplar in many interpersonal dimensions, one is wise to look beyond Boyd, but as Anthony DeLellis observes, "it is possible for people to respect someone who displays some values that are important to them but fails to display others."[40] With that perspective in mind, Boyd does demonstrate that principled leadership requires commitment to something bigger than yourself. In Boyd's case, that meant faithfully pursuing change to a powerful and firmly entrenched status quo, even if the cost was forgoing personal recognition and promotion.

Hugh Thompson and My Lai

Principle: "These people were looking at me for help and there was no way I could turn my back on them."

Lesson: The influence of a principled leader can be both direct and immediate as well as indirect and delayed.

On March 16, 1968, U.S. Army soldiers killed several hundred unarmed people in the Vietnamese village of My Lai. Warrant Officer Hugh Thompson, Jr., and his crew members Glenn Andreotta and Lawrence Colburn were flying a close-air support mission over the village and landed to help wounded civilians they had observed from the air. Once on the ground, Thompson realized a massacre was occurring, and he confronted the perpetrators and brought it to a halt. Thompson was initially ostracized and slandered as various army officials tried to cover up the war crime, and it was not until 1998 that Thompson, Andreotta, and Colburn received Soldier's Medals "for heroism above and beyond the call of duty while saving the lives of at least 10 Vietnamese civilians during the unlawful massacre of non-combatants by American forces at My Lai."

During the Tet Offensive in January 1968, U.S. forces had been attacked by Viet Cong that intelligence reports believed had taken refuge in the Son My, a collection of small hamlets including My Lai, Co Luy, My Khe, and Tu Cung. The place the Americans called "My Lai" was actually called "Tu Cung" by the people who lived there.[41] At about 7:30 a.m. on March 16, some 100 soldiers of Company C, First Battalion, 20th Infantry Regiment, 11th Infantry Brigade, 23rd (Americal) Infantry Division, commanded by Captain Ernest Medina, landed in helicopters at Son My. Wanton and indiscriminate killings began almost immediately. Among the most egregious was when 1st Platoon, led by Lieutenant William Calley, rounded up approximately

75 villagers in an irrigation ditch where they were shot on Calley's orders. The killings continued until as many as 504 Vietnamese were dead.[42]

Thompson was an H-23 pilot from Stone Mountain, Georgia. The H-23 was a light observation helicopter known as a "bubble ship." As Thompson flew over My Lai, he spotted the bodies Calley and his men had shot in the irrigation ditch. Receiving no enemy fire and having seen only one military-age Vietnamese male with a weapon, Thompson could not understand the large number of dead bodies. He radioed a fellow pilot that "it looks to me like there's an awful lot of unnecessary killing going on down there. Something ain't right about this. There's bodies everywhere. There's a ditch full of bodies that we saw. There's something wrong here." As Thompson continued his flight pattern, he saw more bodies and more wounded. He decided to land his helicopter and check things out for himself.[43]

Thompson had a reputation as "an exceptional pilot who took danger in his stride." Although he ruthlessly pursued genuine enemy, Thompson was also "a very moral man ... [who] was absolutely strict about opening fire only on clearly defined targets." He insisted that his gunners see a weapon before opening fire and refused to follow the common practice of assuming a fleeing person must be enemy.[44]

Once on the ground, Thompson made his way toward a wounded woman he had seen from the air. As he did, he encountered Staff Sergeant David Mitchell, the platoon sergeant of First Platoon, C Company. "Sergeant, I see there's some wounded in there. Those people need help," Thompson began. "Any way y'all could help 'em out?" "Yeah," said Mitchell, "we can help them out. We can help put 'em out of their misery." Moments later, Calley arrived and Thompson asked him, "What's going on here, lieutenant?" Calley told Thompson that "this is my show. I'm in charge here. It ain't your concern" and that Thompson "better get back in that chopper and mind your own business." Thompson complied but warned Calley, "you ain't heard the last of this."[45]

As Thompson flew away, his crew chief, Specialist Four Glenn Andreota, shouted, "My God! They're firing into the ditch!" Thompson and his crew flew around for about 10 more minutes trying to figure out what to do. Then Thompson announced, "We're going in." "We're with you, boss," replied door gunner Specialist Four Larry Colburn. "Let's do it." Thompson landed, and as he prepared to dismount, he told Colburn and Andreotta, "Y'all cover me! If these bastards open up on me or these people, you open up on them. Promise me." "You got it, boss," said Colburn.[46]

Thompson walked directly to Lieutenant Stephen Brooks, the platoon leader of Second Platoon, and told him, "Hey, listen, hold your fire. I'm going to try to get these people out of the bunker. Just hold your men there." "Yeah, we can help get 'em out of that bunker—with a hand grenade," replied Brooks. Undeterred, Thompson told him, "Just hold your men there. I think I can do better than that." Noticing that Colburn had his M-60 machine gun trained on them, Brooks and his men stayed put while Thompson patiently coaxed two women, five children, and two elderly men from the bunker.[47]

Because his H-23 had no room for passengers, Thompson radioed for help. Soon, UH-1 pilots Danny Millians and Brian Livingston responded and began shuttling the civilians to safety in an open field about two or three miles from My Lai. With the evacuation complete, Thompson also flew off to refuel, but as he did, Andreotta saw something moving. "Can you swing back around?" he asked Thompson. When Thompson landed, he and Colburn provided security while Andreotta carefully made his way to where he had seen the movement. There, he found a five- or six-year-old boy covered with blood and in shock. Andreotta carefully carried him to the helicopter, and Thompson piloted them to the hospital at Quang Ngai. There, a Catholic nun took the boy into her care, and Thompson flew back to his base.[48]

Soon after landing, Thompson reported what he had seen at My Lai to his platoon leader, Captain Barry Lloyd. Next, Thompson found his company commander, Major Fred Walke. Walke informed Lieutenant Colonel Frank Barker who commanded the task force operating in My Lai. Barker ordered Medina to cease firing immediately.[49] With that, reportedly Medina said, "The party's over."[50]

As soon as the killing stopped, the cover-up began. It actually had already begun shortly before 8:00 a.m. when Michael Bilton and

Kevin Sim assert that Medina told "his first lie of the day" that there were 15 confirmed Viet Cong killed.[51] As the morning progressed, when Medina was asked by the brigade executive officer if any civilians had been killed, Medina reported that a few had been hit by helicopter gunships and artillery fire.[52] Later, when Lieutenant Colonel Barker landed and talked with Medina, Medina stuck to his story that between 20 and 28 civilians had been killed by gunship or artillery fire. By that time, Bilton and Sim note that Medina must "have seen at least a hundred bodies" and that "there had been no firefight and not a single shot had been fired at his men."[53] Later in the day around 4:00 p.m., Medina even repeated the lie to Major General Samuel Koster, the Americal Division commander.[54]

On November 24, Secretary of the Army Stanley Resor appointed Lieutenant General William Peers to conduct a second investigation of My Lai. Peers not only concluded that members of Task Force Barker had "massacred" at least 175 and perhaps more than 400 noncombatants but also that there had been an extensive cover-up throughout the Americal Division.[55] Peers reported that "based on his observations, WO1 Thompson made a specific complaint through his command channels that serious war crimes had been committed but through a series of inadequate responses at each level of command, action on his complaint was delayed and the severity of his charges considerably diluted by the time it reached the Division Commander." Peers declared that the investigation ordered by Koster "was little more than a pretense and was subsequently misrepresented as a thorough investigation to the CG [Commanding General], Americal Division in order to conceal from him the true enormity of the atrocities." Nonetheless, the "patently inadequate reports of investigation submitted by the commander of the 11th Brigade were accepted at face value and without an effective review by the CG, Americal Division."[56] Peers concluded that "at every command level within the Americal Division, actions were taken, both wittingly and unwittingly, which effectively suppressed information concerning the war crimes committed at Son My Village."[57]

On November 17, 1970, a court-martial charged 14 officers with offenses relating to My Lai. Only Calley was convicted. He was found guilty of the premeditated murder of 22 civilians and sentenced to life imprisonment. Nonetheless, there was tremendous support for Calley. Within 24 hours, the White House reported receiving over 5,510 telegrams, of which only five supported the verdict. Of more than 3,000 phone calls, 99 percent opposed the verdict.[58] Under such pressure, President Richard Nixon ordered the Pentagon to release Calley from the stockade and place him under house arrest.

In remarkable contrast to the popular support for Calley, Thompson was characterized as a villain by many. One anonymous letter that typified such sentiment decried Thompson as a "chicken-livered traitor" and a "rat commie."[59] Thompson recalls walking into an Officers' Club only to have everyone turn their backs to him. He noted that it was as if he, not Calley and his soldiers, had committed some kind of atrocity.[60] The army did see fit to award Thompson the Distinguished Flying Cross, but because it falsely referred to Thompson as being caught in a crossfire between U.S. and enemy soldiers, Thompson considered it just another part of the cover-up and threw it away.[61] It was not until 1996, in response to a vigorous campaign by Professor David Egan who had learned of Thompson's heroism from *Remembering My Lai,* a documentary that aired on the Public Broadcasting System, that Thompson and his crew were more appropriately recognized. On March 6, 1998, Thompson, Colburn, and Andreotta (posthumously) were awarded Soldier's Medals, the army's highest award for heroism not involving conflict with an enemy.[62]

Thompson clearly acted according to principles at My Lai, but principled leadership requires more than just individual action. It requires influencing others. Thompson obviously influenced others that day in 1968, but his influence extended far beyond that. During the presentation of the Soldier's Medals, Major General Michael Ackerman addressed that enduring influence, noting that Thompson, Colburn, and Andreotta "set the standards for all soldiers to follow." The investigation that resulted from their actions caused the army "to look at itself and take corrective action to ensure My Lai would never happen again."[63] Colonel Tom Kolditz, head of the United States Military Academy's Behavioral Sciences and Leadership Department, would later explain that "there are so many people today walking around alive because of [Thompson], not only in Vietnam, but people who kept their units under control under other circumstances because they heard his story. We may never know just how many lives he saved."[64] Thompson showed that the influence of a principled leader can be both direct and indirect.

Religious Leaders

Daniel, Shadrach, Meshach, and Abednego and Fixed Principles

Principle: Serve and worship God alone.

Lesson: The fixed and objective nature of principles provides clarity and constancy amid change.

From 605 to 562 BC, Nebuchadnezzar reigned over the Neo-Babylonian Empire. After defeating an Egyptian army at Carchemish in 605, he began extracting tribute from King Jehoiakim of Judah. Nebuchadnezzar also ordered into his service "some of the Israelites from the royal family and the nobility—young men without any physical defect, handsome, showing aptitude for every kind of learning, well informed, quick to understand, and qualified to serve in the king's palace."[1] Among them were Daniel, Shadrach, Meshach, and Abednego. These four men repeatedly showed great moral and physical courage in remaining true to their principle to serve and worship only the God of Israel in spite of changes occurring all around them.

The Israelites chosen to serve Nebuchadnezzar were trained for three years, during which time they received "a daily amount of food and wine from the king's table."[2] Such provisions, however, were contrary to the dietary laws found in Leviticus and other of the laws of Moses. Demonstrating the "precommitment strategy" explained in this book's discussion of Mahatma Gandhi, Daniel had "resolved not to defile himself with the royal food and wine." Therefore, he asked the chief official for permission to eat only vegetables and drink only water. Daniel proposed a test of 10 days, after which time the official could "compare our appearance with that of the young men who eat the royal food, and treat your servants in accordance with what you see." At the end of the test period, Daniel, Shadrach, Meshach, and Abednego "looked healthier and better than any of the young men who ate the royal food. So the guard took away their choice food and the wine that they were to drink and gave them vegetables instead."[3]

Daniel accepted considerable risk in following his principle to obey the dietary laws. When Daniel first made the proposal, the chief official was reluctant to violate the king's instructions. If Daniel ended up "looking worse than the other young men your age," the official protested, "the king would have my head because of you."[4] Thus, when Daniel told the official to "treat your servants in accordance with what you see" after the 10-day test, he was putting himself at the official's mercy. Surely, Daniel must have expected to be treated very harshly if the official felt the experiment failed and his own life was in danger. The safe course would have been for Daniel to simply eat the royal food. After all, he was in captivity and could easily have rationalized that he had no choice in the matter. Instead, he followed a principle to which he had precommitted regardless of the risk to his own safety.

Whereas Daniel was the leader in this case, the next test of principle fell to Shadrach, Meshach, and Abednego at a time when Daniel was at some other unknown location. Nebuchadnezzar had erected a huge gold image and commanded all his subjects that "as soon as you hear the sound of the horn, flute, zither, lyre, harp, pipe, and all kinds of music, you must fall down and worship the image of gold that King Nebuchadnezzar has set up." The punishment for disobedience was to "immediately be thrown into a blazing furnace."[5]

In spite of this threat, Shadrach, Meshach, and Abednego refused to follow the decree. When this fact was reported to Nebuchadnezzar, he was "furious with rage" and demanded the three men be brought before him. He warned them that "if you are ready to fall down and worship the image I made, very good. But if you do not worship it, you will be thrown immediately into a blazing furnace." Even in the face of such a threat, Shadrach, Meshach, and Abednego refused to obey. They told Nebuchadnezzar that "we do not need to defend ourselves before you in this matter. If we are thrown into the blazing furnace, the God we serve is able to deliver us from it, and he will deliver us from Your Majesty's hand. But even if he does not, we want you to know, Your Majesty, that we will not serve your gods or worship the image of gold you have set up."[6]

Stephen Covey notes that principles are "impersonal, factual, objective, and self-evident."[7] Shadrach, Meshach, and Abednego seem to share this belief when they refuse to defend themselves to Nebuchadnezzar. To them, the principle is self-evident and completely independent of whether Nebuchadnezzar subscribes to it or not. Obeying the principle is also an end unto itself rather than a means to another end. Shadrach, Meshach, and Abednego acknowledge that God can save them, but "even if he does not," the principle is still to be followed. The men are so committed to the principle that even Nebuchadnezzar marvels they are "willing to give up their lives rather than serve or worship any god except their own God."[8]

Nebuchadnezzar was succeeded by his son Awel-Marduk who was followed by several other rulers as the Babylonian Empire steadily declined. When the last ruler, Belshazzar, was killed, Darius the Mede came to power. Through all these changes, Daniel remained in his position in the royal court and so impressed Darius "by his exceptional qualities that the king planned to set him over the whole kingdom."[9] Perhaps Daniel's success made his fellow administrators and satraps jealous because they conspired to try to find grounds to bring charges of corruption or negligence against him. They could find nothing and concluded that "we will never find any basis for charges against this man Daniel unless it has something to do with the law of his God."[10]

To that end, the officials tried to set a trap for Daniel. They convinced Darius to issue an edict "that anyone who prays to any god or human being during the next thirty days, except to you, Your Majesty, shall be thrown into the lion's den."[11] Even though Daniel knew of the decree, "three times a day he got down on his knees and prayed, giving thanks to his God, just as he had done before."[12] The conspirators gleefully reported this violation to Darius who reluctantly ordered Daniel to be thrown into the lion's den. When Daniel emerged unharmed the next day, he explained to Darius that "I was found innocent in [God's] sight."[13] In seeing Daniel safe, Darius was "overjoyed" and issued a new decree "that in every part of my kingdom people must fear and reverence the God of Daniel."[14]

Using language consistent with Stephen Covey, David Guralnik describes principles as being "fixed, invariable, absolute, eternal." Unlike values, they are not subject to change.[15] Thus, even though Darius decreed a new value in Babylonian society, Daniel held to his principle and continued to pray to God "just as he had before."[16] Unlike Daniel, Darius was a man of values, not principles. One moment, he issued a decree declaring that no one can pray to any god or human except Darius. The next moment, he declared everyone must fear and reverence the God of Daniel. Darius, in reversing his decree, demonstrates the changing nature of values. Daniel, in continuing to pray to God, demonstrates the unchanging nature of principles.

Daniel, Shadrach, Meshach, and Abednego faced several challenges to their principle to serve and worship only the God of Israel. Changes in their circumstances, in the whims of rulers, in their safety, in societal values and norms all mattered not. Because principles are fixed and objective, the four men had a constant in the midst of the changes occurring all around them. This clarity guided their decision-making and actions regardless of the situational variables.

Thich Quang Do and Speaking Truth to Power

Principle: "Then and there I vowed to do all that I could to combat fanaticism and intolerance and devote my life to the pursuit of justice through the Buddhist teachings of nonviolence, tolerance and compassion."[17]

Lesson: Speak truth to power in a virtuous way.

James O'Toole writes, "Speaking truth to power is perhaps the oldest and, certainly, one of the most difficult of ethical challenges because to do so entails personal danger."[18] Thich Quang Do was a Vietnamese Buddhist monk who for many years spoke the truth about oppression and freedom to both the democratic and communist governments in power in Vietnam. O'Toole argues that speaking truth to power can sometimes be inappropriate or harmful. For the act to be considered virtuous, O'Toole requires that

1. it has to be truthful;
2. it must do no harm to innocents;
3. it must not be self-interested (the benefits must go to others or to the organization);
4. it must be the product of moral reflection;
5. the messenger must be willing to pay the price; and
6. it must not be done out of spite or anger.[19]

Do's speaking truth to power is an example of a principled leader meeting all of O'Toole's criteria.

O'Toole's first criterion is that the speech must be truthful. In 1995, Ngo Dinh Diem became the president of South Vietnam. Diem was a Catholic and had been educated in French schools. He was overtly hostile to the Buddhists that made up as high as 90 percent of South Vietnam's population, giving preference to Catholics in public service and the military, land distribution, business, and taxes. Such policies precipitated the "Buddhist crisis" that was sparked in May 1963 when nine civilians were shot while protesting Diem's ban on public display of the Buddhist flag. The government was so hardened in its attitude that when Buddhist monk Thich Quang Duc self-immolated to protest the policies, Diem's sister-in-law declared, "If the Buddhists wish to have another barbecue, I will be glad to supply the gasoline and a match."[20] It was under these circumstances that Do first began to speak truth to power.

After the Communist victory in the Vietnam War, Buddhist persecution continued in the Socialist Republic of Vietnam. Since 1965, Do had served as the secretary-general of the Viện Hóa Đạo (Institute for the Dissemination of Dharma) of the Unified Buddhist Church of Vietnam (UBCV). The Communist government quickly moved to suppress Buddhism, confiscating UBCV property, dismantling its institutions, and arresting or forcing into military service thousands of monks. In an effort to control the Buddhist population, in 1981, the government created the state-sponsored Vietnam Buddhist Church and declared it the sole representative of Vietnamese Buddhism both in the country and abroad. In 2019, the United States Commission on International Religious Freedom, an independent, bipartisan federal government commission that monitors the universal right to freedom of religion or belief abroad, recommended Vietnam be designated as a "country of particular concern ... for engaging in systematic, ongoing, and egregious religious freedom violations, as defined by the International Religious Freedom Act."[21] From the 1960s until his death, Do certainly was being truthful when he spoke against Buddhist repression in Vietnam.

O'Toole's second criterion is that the speech must do no harm to innocents. Do was careful not to place his fellow Vietnamese citizens in danger as he struggled on their behalf. "People are very afraid of the government," he told the Associated Press in a rare 2003 interview. "Only I dare to say what I want to say. That is why they are afraid of me."[22] Do even refused to cause harm to his enemies. In an open letter to Communist Party secretary-general Do Muoi in 1994, Do declared a lifelong commitment to "combat fanaticism and intolerance" but to do so "through the Buddhist teachings of non-violence, tolerance and compassion."[23]

O'Toole's third criterion is that the speech must not be self-interested. The benefits from it must go to others or to the organization. What Do did, he did on behalf of the Vietnamese people. He explained that his church was interested in human rights and democracy "because we see the Vietnamese people in general are very, very miserable because they have to live under a dictator, a regime. All their rights are taken away, they have nothing." He said that the UBCV "made up our minds—we must do something to change the situation. That's why we continue to do what we do now." "As long as the Vietnamese people suffer," Do vowed, "we suffer with them. That's why we continue our fight until Vietnam has freedom, democracy, and peace."[24]

O'Toole's fourth criterion is that the speech must be the product of moral reflection. Do captured the results of his moral reflection by publishing his "Appeal for Democracy in Vietnam" in 2001. This eight-point declaration called for a multiparty system, free elections, independent trade unions, and the abolition of "all degrading forms of imported culture and ideologies that pervert Vietnamese spiritual and moral values."[25] Beyond these basic appeals for human rights,

Do's moral reflection included a commitment to Buddhism's "*nemah,*" which he explained as "the law [that] everything is changing." Because of this "impermanence," Do believed that "at last the Communists will have an end.... That's why I think in the long run Vietnam will become a free and democratic country, and at that time the Vietnamese people will be happy."[26] Moral reflection gave Do both the justification for his speech and the confidence that it will eventually bear fruit.

O'Toole's fifth criterion is that the messenger must be willing to pay the price. Do was first imprisoned in 1963 for his activism against Diem's anti–Buddhist policies. Do was released after the fall of the Diem regime in November, but his health had suffered from the torture and poor conditions, and he had contracted tuberculosis.[27] After the Communists came to power, Do continued to advocate for human rights and spent most of the last 30 years of his life in and out of prison, under house arrest, or forced into internal exile for refusing to submit the UBCV to government control.[28] In 1977, he was arrested on charges of "undermining national solidarity" and conducting "anti-revolutionary activities" and was forced to spend nearly two years of solitary confinement in a roughly three-by-six-foot prison cell until international pressure forced his release. In 1982, Do was again arrested for resisting efforts to force the UBCV to join the state-run Vietnam Buddhist Church. He was sent into internal exile in the remote village of Vu Doai, where he spent 10 years under house arrest. His 84-year-old mother was exiled with him, and she died in 1985 from malnutrition and lack of medical care. In 1995, Do was sentenced to five years in prison and five years of house arrest on charges of "sabotaging national solidarity" and "taking advantage of democratic freedoms to violate the interests of the State and social organizations" stemming from an altercation with the government over a UBCV flood relief effort.[29] International pressure led to his early release in 1998, but he was again placed under house arrest in 2001. He was released in 2003 but endured various forms of surveillance, internal exile, house arrest, or government harassment until his death in 2020.[30]

O'Toole's sixth criterion is that the speech must not be done out of spite or anger. Do's adherence to this requirement is perhaps the most remarkable aspect of his story. He declared, "In my mind, I have no hate. No hate. I try to create my feelings to love everyone." When asked if he forgives the Vietnamese government, he said he does and when asked why, he explained, "Because they are also men. I want—the only thing I want from the Communists—is to turn their ideas, to give up their communism … and realize democracy and freedom and human rights for all Vietnamese people and them they will be happy."

Do explained that he has been placed in isolation "because the Communist government here thinks that if I am free as everyone else is I will continue my fight for freedom and democracy. That is why they put me under house arrest so that I have no opportunity of meeting many people. Here if I speak I have no one to speak with or if anyone comes to see me sometimes the police is there, over there, across the street and they come in." The Oslo Freedom Forum echoes that "the communist government has sought to render [Do] silent and invisible to the outside world."[31]

Do died in 2020 while under house arrest at the Tu Hieu Pagoda in Ho Chi Minh City. He was nominated for the Nobel Peace Prize nine times[32] and received a number of human rights awards, including Norway's Rafto Prize in 2006, which cited "his personal courage and perseverance through three decades of peaceful opposition against the Communist regime in Vietnam."[33] During those three decades, Do served as a powerful example of how a principled leader speaks truth to power.

Father Damien and the Leper Colony at Kalaupapa

Principle: "I would like to sacrifice myself for the poor lepers."[34]

Lesson: Servant leadership and principled leadership are not the same thing, but there are points of intersection.

Servant leadership is a leadership approach in which the leader meets the subordinate's legitimate needs—which might include such concerns as training, encouragement, resources, or help with personal issues—in order to allow the subordinate to better focus on and accomplish the organizational mission.[35] Many leadership theorists have identified a relationship between servant leadership and principled leadership. For example, servant leadership was one of the four value-based leadership theories Karen Hendrikz and Amos Engelbrecht integrated to develop their "construct" of principled leadership. They explain that servant leadership "has strong links to the universal principles of being committed to something greater than oneself and caring for others."[36] This theme is also found in the foreword to Robert Greenleaf's seminal *Servant Leadership*, where Stephen Covey identifies moral authority as "the core of servant leadership." Covey continues to say that "the essence of moral authority or conscience is sacrifice—the subordinating of one's self or one's ego to a higher purpose, cause, or principle."[37] Elsewhere, Covey identifies one of the characteristics of being a principle-centered leader as being "service-oriented."[38] Father Damien, who ministered from 1873 until his death in 1889 at the leper colony on the Kalaupapa Peninsula of the Hawaiian island of Molokai, is an example of this connection between servant leadership and principled leadership.

The man who would become Father Damien was born Jozef ("Jef") De Veuster in Belgium in 1840. At age 18, De Veuster committed himself to a religious calling, and he joined his older brother Pamphile at the Fathers of the Sacred Heart of Jesus and Mary at Louvain. When Pamphile was precluded from going to Hawai'i as a missionary because of illness, Jozef went in his place. He arrived at Honolulu Harbor on March 19, 1864, and was ordained into the priesthood in the Cathedral of Our Lady of Peace on May 21 and took the name of Damien.

Leprosy reached epidemic proportions in Hawai'i in the late 1800s, a time when there was no known cure or treatment for the disease. Hoping to stem the spread, in 1865, the Legislative Assembly passed, and King Kamehameha V approved, the Act to Prevent the Spread of Leprosy, which required the most serious leprosy cases to be relocated to a settlement colony at the village Kalawao on the eastern end of the remote Kalaupapa Peninsula on the island of Molokai.

On January 6, 1866, the first group of nine men and three women was dropped off on the peninsula. By October, there were 101 men and 41 women at Kalawao. It was expected that the colonists would be able to farm and become self-sustaining. Instead, a variety of obstacles, not the least of which was their medical condition, made such an ambitious scheme impractical, and the colonists suffered horribly.[39] The National Park Service history of Kalaupapa reports that the colonists "had been left to die."[40]

Damien's first posting was to the Catholic Mission in North Kohala on the island of Hawai'i. It was there that he was first exposed to the condition of Hawai'i's lepers and saw government authorities round them up to be sent into isolation.[41] Fathers Raymond, Albert, and Boniface had all made short stays at Molokai to minister to the colonists, but new Board of Health regulations now required any future minister to remain in Molokai for life. Four priests, including Damien, volunteered for the assignment, and Damien was selected by Louis-Désiré Maigret, the vicar apostolic of the Sandwich Islands.[42]

Servant leaders serve voluntarily. They do so by choice. Sen Sendjaya and his colleagues identify "voluntary subordination" as one of the "conceptual dimensions of servant leadership." They explain that "central to servant leadership is a willingness to take up opportunities to serve others whenever there is a legitimate need regardless of the nature of the service, the person served, or the mood of the servant leader."[43] Indeed, when Damien volunteered, Maigret told him that "this employment is of such a nature that I would not have imposed it on anyone, but I gladly accept your offer."[44]

The inter-island steamer *Kilauca* was soon departing for Molokai with 50 lepers, and Damien saw the opportunity to act quickly. He had time only to get one extra shirt and his breviary before setting sail.[45] Maigret accompanied Daimen to Molokai, and when Damien first saw the pitiful conditions of the lepers there, Maigret offered him the opportunity to reconsider his decision. Damien resolved to stay, explaining in a letter a week later that "I would like to sacrifice myself for the poor lepers. The harvest seems ripe here."[46] Maigret left him with this introduction to his new companions: "So far, my children, you have been left alone and uncared for. But you shall be so no longer. I have brought you one who will be a father to you, and who loves you so much that for your welfare and for the sake of your immortal souls, he does not hesitate to become one of you; to live and die with you."[47] It was May 10, 1873.

Damien found the colonists living in primitive huts that offered little shelter.[48] The conditions were so deplorable that the average life span of a leper after arriving at Molokai was estimated to be between three and four years.[49] Damien's biographer John Farrow notes, though, that "almost as depressing as the visible effect of the disease was the air of hopelessness and fear that permeated the entire settlement."[50] Damien would bring hope.

Damien's first act was to begin cleaning up St. Philomena Church, which had been built by the colonists in 1872, but he was soon asked to officiate the burial of a leper who had died the previous day. Damien found there was little dignity involved in such proceedings. The deceased was wrapped in a piece of old matting and buried in a shallow ditch just deep enough to cover the corpse. Packs of wild dogs and pigs later would roam through the fenceless cemetery, digging up remains.[51] As Damien returned to the village, an old woman pleaded with him to minister to her Catholic son who was dying. As he pronounced the last rites, Damien found worms gnawing away at the man's foot.[52] Damien's earliest moments on the island laid bare to him the horrors of the colony.

Damien soon began meeting a host of needs. Noticing that scarce water was collected in various small vessels and carried by hand from distant gulches, Damien devised a plan to deliver abundant fresh water from a natural reservoir. He petitioned the government to send the necessary piping, but his requests were initially ignored. He then launched a "relentless barrage of reports and complaints" to the Board of Health that eventually yielded a shipment of pipes. Before long, the colonists had a convenient and reliable source of water. "The long weary pilgrimages to the distant springs were suddenly ceased before this miracle of the faucet," Farrow writes, "and grateful eyes, alight with a new respect, were turned on this man whose pity for them had so strongly practical a bent."[53]

Other times, Damien traveled to Honolulu to advocate for supplies. He met indifference and resistance, and in a move that eliminated Damien's means of transportation, the president of the Board of Health denied access to a ship anchored offshore to anyone in the colony. Damien was destined to continue to fight the bureaucracy the rest of his life.[54]

Damien did succeed in convincing his bishop to send building materials and tools, and even the Board of Health, under pressure from the public, arranged for a shipment of lumber. The colonists used these supplies to build new cottages for themselves, each built on solid trestles to withstand storms, placed in orderly rows, and neatly whitewashed. Soon they planted gardens of vegetables and flowers in their yards.[55] Damien led in a way that encouraged the colonists to invest in their own situations and to improve their conditions.[56]

In addition to the deplorable physical conditions, Damien soon found that "the morals of the colony were as unhealthy and viciously bad as they could be." He reported that "vice reigned instead of virtue. When new lepers came, the old ones were eager to impress upon them with the principle: *aole kanawai ma keia wahi*—'In this place there is no law.'"[57] Under such conditions, the weak were particularly vulnerable. Drunkenness and licentiousness flourished. Slowly but surely, Damien began to reverse this atmosphere. His efforts were not always well received. Farrow notes that Damien "was of a race which [the colonists] rightly blamed not only for their disease but also for the laws of banishment to Molokai, and when he started to campaign against the regime of vice he was met with open resistance."[58] Using both persuasion and authority, Damien made progress. Farrow reports that Damien's "flair for leadership and his executive ability succeeded in bringing discipline and order to the settlement for the first time, something that the Government with all threats of armed forces had been unable to do."[59]

Damien served by being completely immersed in the colony and its people. Rather than avoiding contact, Damien deliberately made it a point to eat from the same dishes as infected people, and he often shared his pipe with a leper.[60] He led by example. Unless he was engaged in a priestly duty, Farrow reports that Damien "was never to be seen without a hammer, plane or tool of some description in his hand." He could be found everywhere, "exhorting and urging, keeping the flame of enthusiasm at a high pitch."[61] "I make myself a leper with the lepers to gain all to Jesus Christ," Damien said. "That is why, in preaching, I say 'we lepers,' not, 'my brethren.'"[62]

In 1885, Damien noticed the first signs of leprosy in himself. Still, he labored on, assisted now by two other priests and two laymen. Damien died on April 15, 1889. He had served 15 years at Molokai and was 49 years old. He was canonized by the Catholic Church on October 11, 2009. This renewed interest in Damien led to his approach to leprosy being cited as a positive example for how to humanely treat similar marginalized groups, especially those with HIV/AIDS.[63] Among his champions was President Barack Obama who declared that "as millions around the world suffer from disease, especially the pandemic of HIV/AIDS, we should draw on the example of Father Damien's resolve in answering the urgent call to heal and care for the sick."[64]

Although servant leadership and principled leadership may be compatible, they are not the same thing. Among their points of intersection is the idea of subordinating one's self to something greater. In servant leadership, that means the needs of others. In principled leadership, it means principles. In some cases, the two align, such as in Damien's principle of serving others. Still, if principled leadership is to warrant consideration as a unique leadership theory, it would seem that it must be more than just a construct of servant leadership and three other theories as Hendrikz and Engelbrecht posit, and principled leaders must be oriented on more than just service and the other characteristics listed by Covey. The Introduction of this book defined principled leadership as "the process of using principles as the means of influencing others to accomplish goals that optimize those principles, even at the expense of other considerations." It defined servant leadership as "a leadership approach in which the leader meets the subordinate's legitimate needs ... in order to allow the subordinate to better focus on and accomplish the organizational mission." Damien was both a principled and a servant leader.

James and the Jerusalem Council

Principle: "The remnant of men may seek the Lord, and all the Gentiles who bear my name, says the Lord, who does these things that have been known for ages."[65]

Lesson: When it comes to compromise, context matters. Compromising in a relationship may be good, but compromising principles is not.

In the early decades after the death of Jesus, controversy arose between the Judaizers and the more liberal wing of the Christian church at Antioch in Syria. The key players in the drama are Paul who was the principle missionary to the Gentile Christians, Peter who focused on the Jewish Christians, and James who was the brother of Jesus and the leader of the church in Jerusalem. The main issue revolved around circumcision and whether the Gentile Christians were obligated to fulfill this aspect of Mosaic law. A crisis arose in Antioch where Paul accused Peter of hypocrisy by "separat[ing] himself from the Gentiles because he was afraid of those who belonged to the circumcision group."[66] This latter group purported to be representatives of James and told the Gentiles that "unless you are circumcised, according to the custom taught by Moses, you cannot be saved." The dissension and debate became so intense that Paul, Barnabas, and some others were appointed "to go up to Jerusalem to see the apostles and elders about this question."[67]

Manuel London argues that "principled leaders act in a diplomatic way to make decisions, resolve conflict, and negotiate agreements."[68] They seek "positive" outcomes that involve "everyone [being] pleased with the end result," "everyone leaving [with the] feeling they had achieved an important part of their goal," and "participants compromis[ing]."[69] It is easy to imagine how such considerations, especially compromise, might result in a deviation from pure principles. This danger was what James faced as the various stakeholders presented their cases in this situation.

Jesus was a Jew, and Christianity emerged from Judaism as a new religion that accepted Jesus as Messiah. The earliest Christians were Jews, and the vast majority of the first converts were Jewish. A Gentile is a non–Jewish person. Gentile conversion to Christianity began slowly, but soon a consciously Gentile outreach program began with its center at Antioch. Barnabas was originally recruited to lead this effort, and he immediately had Paul join him in the work. Antioch then became the center of a more widespread missionary effort, beginning with Paul and Barnabas's missionary journey to Cyprus, Asia Minor, and back to Antioch. The success of Paul's missionary efforts changed the proportions so that new Christians were increasingly converted Gentiles rather than Jews. According to Stanley Porter, "The prospect of Gentile Christianity becoming a sizeable group, possibly even the majority of those who followed Jesus as savior, raised questions about the very nature of this newly formed group called Christians."[70]

In addition to these Gentile converts, another group with which James had to contend were the Judaizers, a section of Jewish Christians who believed that the Old Testament Levitical laws were still binding on all Christians.[71] It is easy to dismiss the Judaizers as self-serving agitators, but T.C. Smith offers a balanced, yet circumspect, assessment. Smith notes that

> circumcision and the convert's obligation by that act to observe the Mosaic law gave promise of a lesser degree of immorality among Gentile Christians. Coming out of a pagan background, without a moral standard to restrain them, the Gentile Christians were always in danger of reverting to their former sinful manner of life. The circumcision party feared that this might happen and that the whole Christian community would be dragged down to the level of Gentile immorality.

In spite of this sympathetic rendering, Smith concludes that "the real basis of [the Judaizers'] reaction stemmed from prejudice and narrow provincialism."[72]

The third group before James were the Pharisees, a religious and political group that had often been at odds with Jesus over issues of ritual purity and Sabbath observance. They followed both the written law and their own oral traditions that laid the foundation for what would become rabbinical Judaism. The Pharisaical converts continued to follow the Jewish law and believed that all followers of Jesus had to become Jews. This belief would put the Pharisees in agreement with the Judaizers about circumcision.[73]

As the various points of view were presented in Jerusalem, James quietly listened.[74] Much was at stake. The circumcision controversy posed the very real possibility of a split in the church. If James decided to impose Jewish law on the Gentiles, the church at Antioch could have conceivably separated from the church in Jerusalem and formed their own Christian church. It was also possible that the Gentiles could leverage their increasing numbers to demand that their approach to following Christ become the norm for all Christians. Jewish Christians would likely respond to this outcome either by ostracizing the Gentile Christians or even reverting to Judaism without Christ. Because of the difficulty in resolving the matter, James may have been tempted to ignore it for the time being, hoping that it might somehow resolve itself. Seeming to appreciate that left to itself, the situation would only worsen, James determined to settle the matter.[75]

Smith notes that "people generally get apprehensive when their traditional viewpoints are challenged, unless they are ... competent to test new insights."[76] Porter writes that in his testing, James might have appealed to "Jewish practice, Jewish (Mosaic) Law, tradition, temporal priority, innovation and development, practical results, popular appeal, convenience, the testimony of the Holy Spirit, God's direct or indirect guidance, or any number of other bases."[77] Instead, James turned to the "words of the prophets" as representative of the scriptural principles on which to base his decision.[78] In the Septuagint version of Amos 9:11–12, James found that "after this I will return and rebuild David's fallen tent. Its ruins I will rebuild, and I will restore it, that the remnant of men may seek the Lord, and all the Gentiles who bear my name, says the Lord, who does these things that have been known for ages." In this passage from Amos, James viewed the present situation not as an isolated incident but as part of a grand plan that had "been known for the ages." James saw the inclusion of the Gentiles into the body of the followers of Jesus as part of a movement of Jewish restoration whose ultimate goal was the betterment of all humanity. Porter describes this movement as progressing "from Jesus to his people the Jews, to the Gentiles, and to the ends of the earth, the restoration and creation of a revitalized and expanded and expanding people of God." James, Porter continues, was saying "that the Jewish

Scriptures themselves foretold that this was the plan that God had in mind." By basing his decision on what is "grounded in God's previous inspired counsel," James was able to resolve a conflict without compromising principle.[79]

According to the principle he found in the book of Amos, James declared, "It is my judgment, therefore, that we should not make it difficult for the Gentiles who are turning to God. Instead we should write to them, telling them to abstain from food polluted by idols, from sexual morality, from meat of strangled animals and from blood."[80] Porter notes that in his decision, James had the wisdom to "impose the minimum, not the maximum."[81]

James began the process of principled leadership described in the Introduction by "reviewing the statements of the principles."[82] For James, those principles were recorded in the Scripture, in this case in the book of Amos. Then James "eliminated all solutions that are inconsistent with the principles."[83] Specifically, that meant anything that would "make it difficult for the Gentiles who are turning to God" because Gentiles had been listed in Amos as being among those who "may seek the Lord." James then decided that the action necessary for the leader was to make a judgment and notify the "Gentile believers in Antioch, Syria and Cilicia" of it by letter.[84]

The letter informed the Gentile Christians of the decision "not to burden you with anything beyond the following requirements: You are to abstain from food sacrificed to idols, from blood, from the meat of strangled animals and from sexual immorality."[85] Why James picked the four conditions he did is a matter of debate that will not be pursued here. What is important for this discussion is that James "chose a minimal solution to secure what he saw as the most desirable outcome, which was the preservation of the unity of the early Christian church."[86] By following the principle found in Amos, James facilitated Gentile conversion to Christianity without impeding the practices of Jewish Christians. Indeed, he closed his decision with a statement recognizing the importance of the Jewish heritage by noting that "Moses has been preached in every city from the earliest times and is read in the synagogues on every Sabbath."[87] By taking the "impose the minimum, not the maximum" approach, James demonstrated Anna

Simons's description of principled leadership as a very empowering form of leadership that makes available to the leader a host of options, so long as they are consistent with the values.[88]

Carrie Menkel-Meadow notes that "*different contexts* clearly produce different assessments of the ethics of compromise" (emphasis original). In relationships, compromise involves considering the needs and interests of "the other" and "giving up" something to someone else because we value that person more than we value the particular issue in dispute. In this context, compromise is generally considered to be good. In philosophy, however, compromise connotes a "giving up" of pure principle and commitment to truth, demonstrating weakness or lack of integrity. Compromising principles demonstrates a lack of integrity and an affront to how a person defines himself or herself.[89] In this context, and in the context of principled leadership, compromise is bad. In resolving the circumcision controversy, James achieved the "positive outcome" sought by Manuel London without compromising principles.

Sports Leaders

Eric Liddell and the 1924 Olympics

Principle: "I object to Sunday sport in toto."[1]

Lesson: Although adherence to principles can come with some costs, it is also very liberating in the sense that it simplifies a leader's decision-making.

An early step in applying the process of principled leadership identified in the Introduction is to eliminate all solutions that are inconsistent with the principles.[2] As a leader does so, he or she often comes face-to-face with the costs that will be incurred by following his or her principles. These may include losses in social standing, economic prosperity, popularity, and comfort. Rather than viewing this condition as a negative, mature principled leaders view it as a liberating step that frees them from distractions standing in their way of achieving a higher purpose. Eric Liddell experienced this liberation as an athlete and a missionary in completely surrendering to his principles.

Liddell was born in Tientsin, China, to missionary parents. At age six, he left China to attend a boarding school in England, and in 1920, he enrolled in the University of Edinburgh. There, Liddell excelled in rugby and track. His best event was the 100-meter race, and in the 1923 British Championships, he set a British record of 9.7 seconds that stood until Peter Radford ran a 9.6 in 1958.

A few months before the 1923 British Championships, Liddell had been invited to speak at an evangelical meeting in the industrial town of Armadale in central Scotland. Up to this point, Liddell's faith had always been a rather private matter, but Julian Wilson identifies the Armadale meeting as a turning point for Liddell. Thence, Wilson argues that Liddell would follow an undeviating path of "the complete surrender of his will to God."[3]

Liddell's commitment to this principle would soon be tested. When the schedule for the 1924 Summer Olympics in Paris was published, Liddell learned that the 100-meter race would be held on July 6, a Sunday. For Liddell, this scheduling created a conflict with the biblical command to "remember the Sabbath day, to keep it holy. Six days you shall labor, and do all your work, but the seventh day is the Sabbath of the Lord your God." Liddell announced that he would not run the 100 meters, telling interviewers, "I object to Sunday sport in toto."[4] Although the movie *Chariots of Fire* depicts Liddell's decision as a last-minute one, in reality, he decided early on that his religious principles would not allow him to run in his best event. When he did, Lord Sands notes, Liddell "put his whole career as a runner in the balance, and deemed it as small dust, compared to remaining true to his principles."[5]

Because Liddell was "Britain's best hope for a gold medal in the 100 metres" in the Olympics, Wilson contends that Liddell's decision not to run "aroused the wrath of a nation."[6] In fact, many of his fellow Britons tried to pressure him to compromise his principles and run. They told Liddell that because the race was not until the afternoon, he would have plenty of time to go to church in the morning. Others suggested "he could worship God in the morning and run to God's glory in the afternoon." Some pointed out that the continental Sabbath lasted only until noon. "Mine," Liddell replied, "lasts all day." Eric Mataxas notes that Liddell "could not compromise on what he believed God had commanded."[7] Instead, Liddell began training for the 400-meter race.

Instead of running in the preliminary heats for his signature event, Liddell spent July 6 in church and later visiting the Tomb of the Unknown Soldier to honor World War I dead with his teammates and the Prince of Wales. The next day, Liddell watched his teammate Harold Abrahams narrowly defeat American Jackson Scholz for the 100-meter gold.[8]

On July 7, Liddell ran in the 200-meter race. He finished third behind Scholz and Charles Paddock. In addition to the 100-meter race, Liddell also gave up running the 4 × 100-meter relay and the 4 × 400-meter relay races because they were held on Sunday, July 13. Instead, he spent that day preaching in Scots Kirk in Paris.[9]

The 400-meter final was held on July 11. Before the race, Liddell was handed a small note that said, "In the old book it says: 'He that honors me, I will honor.' Wishing you the best of success always." *Chariots of Fire* depicts Scholz handing this reference to 1 Samuel 2:30 to Liddell. In actuality, a trainer made the delivery, but the impact was not diminished. "It was perhaps the finest thing I experienced in Paris," Liddell said later, "a great surprise and a great pleasure to know there were others who shared my sentiments about the Lord's day."[10] This is one example of how Liddell's adherence to his principles transcended personal action and entered into the leadership realm of influencing others.

Liddell drew lane six, the outermost lane, for the 400-meter race. This position was considered disadvantageous because starting well in front of the other runners, he would be initially running "blind." Liddell jumped out to an early lead, but many observers expected him to tire toward the end of the race. Instead, he increased his lead, winning by six meters with a world record time of 47.6 seconds. When asked for comment on his victory, Liddell explained his strategy: "The secret of my success over the 400 meter is that I run the first 200 meters as fast as I can. Then, for the second 200 meters, with God's help I run faster."[11] Again, Liddell took the opportunity to influence others by communicating his principle of surrendering to God.

Eric Eichinger writes that Liddell returned from Paris "as a gold medalist and a national hero but—more importantly—as a man who'd stood his ground."[12] Just days later, he graduated from the University of Edinburgh and soon announced he would return to China as a missionary. His first posting was to the Anglo-Chinese College in Tientsin where he ministered to the sons of wealthy Chinese families while teaching science, mathematics, and sports.

In 1934, Liddell married Canadian missionary Florence Mackenzie and the couple had three daughters. On the brink of Japan's invasion of China, the British government ordered its nationals to leave China. Liddell saw his family safely off to Canada but chose to continue his ministry in China. In 1943, Japanese forces captured him and sent him to an internment camp, where he died of a brain tumor on February 21, 1945, just five months before the camp's liberation.

At a camp memorial service on March 3, A.P. Cullen, one of Liddell's friends, summed up his life as being "literally God-controlled, in his thoughts, judgments, actions, words to an extent I have never seen surpassed, and rarely seen equaled."[13] Missionary nurse Annie Buchan was with Liddell as he lay dying. Before he lapsed into a final coma, he told her, "Annie, it's complete surrender." Later, Buchan commented that Liddell "was a man who'd been surrendering to God all his life and I don't believe it cost him much to say 'complete surrender.'"[14]

Other case studies have illustrated how adherence to principles often comes at a cost to the leader. Liddell certainly experienced such costs in forfeiting his chance for 100-meter gold and his health and family in China. Yet the comments of Cullen and Buchan also indicate the liberating aspects of adherence to principles. Such commitment removes from the leader the ambiguities, distractions, competing interests, and temptations that can cloud decision-making and action. For leaders like Liddell, his complete surrender to his principles simplified his life by lending it a laser-like clarity of purpose. It removed from him the "small dust" that Lord Sands alludes to. Liddell considered adherence to his principles to be empowering rather than burdensome. As such, he represents a very high order of commitment to principled leadership.

Bobby Jones and the 1925 U.S. Open

Principle: "There is only one way to play this game."[15]

Lesson: Personal power, earned by the setting of example, is an effective means of influence for the principled leader.

Born on March 17, 1902, in Atlanta, Georgia, Robert Tyre "Bobby" Jones, Jr., was a golf child prodigy, playing in the 1916 U.S. Amateur Tournament when he was just 14 years old. He went on to win 13 major championships, culminating in 1930 when his victories in the

British Amateur, the British Open, the U.S. Open, and the U.S. Amateur Championships won him the "Grand Slam of Golf." But Jones was not only a consummately skilled golfer. Journalist and commentator Alistair Cooke described Jones as "a gentleman, a combination of goodness and grace, an unwavering courtesy, self-deprecation, and consideration for other people."[16] Jones's exemplification of principles relating to sportsmanship and fair play earned him universal renown and helped him transform America's relationship with golf.

Perhaps the most well-known demonstration of Jones's characteristic integrity occurred in the first round of the 1925 U.S. Open at the Worcester Country Club near Boston, Massachusetts. There, Jones's approach shot to the 11th hole's elevated green fell short into the deep rough of the embankment. As Jones prepared to pitch onto the green, the head of his club brushed the grass and caused the ball to move slightly. Jones proceeded to take the shot and then told his playing partner Walter Hagen and the U.S. Golf Association (USGA) official covering their match that he was calling a penalty on himself for violating Rule 18, "Ball at rest moved." Neither Hagen nor the official had seen the ball move, but Jones was insistent. Play continued, and when the round was over but before Jones had signed his scorecard, officials again tried to talk Jones out of imposing the penalty stroke. Jones would not be deterred and recorded a 77 instead of a 76. The one-stroke difference left Jones tied with Willie McFarlane and forced a playoff, which McFarlane won.[17] To a man of principle such as Jones, Stephen Lowe writes that "it seemed honesty and sportsmanship mattered more than money or glory."[18]

It was not until after the tournament that reporters learned that Jones had called the penalty on himself. Although they hailed Jones's honesty, they were also stunned by it. In the 1920s, golf had not yet become popularized as a national sport, and few sportswriters understood its self-refereed protocols. Instead, they were more accustomed to the dirty tricks that abounded in other sports such as pitchers throwing spitballs in baseball. Writers found golf's self-regulation so novel that their coverage of Jones's conduct almost eclipsed the championship itself. They magnified Jones's stature by depicting him not just as a star athlete but as a hero of impeccable virtue and character.

Rather than reveling in the limelight, Jones was chagrined by the press's ignorance of golf's code of honor and their amazement at what he considered to simply be expected behavior. "You'd as well praise me for not breaking into banks," he said.[19]

Jones's integrity was not unique to the 1925 Open. A similar event occurred in the next U.S. Open, played at the Scioto Country Club in Columbus, Ohio. In the second round, Jones found himself in second place and preparing to putt on the 15th green in the face of a strong wind. Jones grounded his putter to square up the club face, and when he lifted the club head to place it behind the ball, the ball rolled a half turn in the wind. As at Worcester, no one else observed this movement of the ball, but again Jones called a penalty on himself. This time, Jones's honesty did not cost him, and he went on to win the second of his four U.S. Open victories. As a result of such character, Michael Schoenecke declares that Jones came to "exemplif[y] golf and honesty."[20]

As impressive as Jones's integrity in these two situations is, in order to elevate it beyond individual excellence and into the realm of principled leadership, there must be some element of influencing others. In *Heroes & Ballyhoo: How the Golden Age of the 1920s Transformed American Sports*, Michael Bohn argues that it was in this period that "sports became a cornerstone of modern American life," and he profiles "the ten most prominent" figures that made this transformation a realty. Jones's contribution, claims Bohn, was to "change golf into a spectator sport."[21] Historian of southern culture Charles Reagan Wilson adds that Jones's impact was particularly pronounced in his native South.[22]

The personal integrity such as Jones displayed in the 1925 U.S. Open captured the imagination of the American public. In the various news outlets, he was frequently referred to as the embodiment of the southern gentleman. Wilson describes Jones as "self-consciously 'southern' in his attitudes" and credits him with "symbolizing a transitional figure—the traditional regional image of the gentleman in a new 20th-century mass culture context."[23]

Jones's personal character affected not just the South but the United States as a whole. Regarding this larger impact, Bohn argues that Jones was part of a phenomenon in the 1920s that saw sports as "helping bond disparate social and regional sectors of the country." Jones served to project a part of what was good about southern culture to the rest of America. Within the South, Jones's status as a native son attracted southerners to the sport. Wilson explains that "although golf was not as popular in the South as in the Northeast and on the West Coast, Jones nonetheless consciously worked to increase its popularity in his home region."[24]

One of Jones's enduring contributions to golf was conceiving and assisting in the design of the Augusta National Golf Course in Augusta, Georgia, home of the Masters Tournament. Jones reports that he developed the idea because "my native Southland, especially my own neighborhood, had very few, if any, golf courses of championship quality." He regarded it "as an opportunity to make a contribution to golf in my own section of the country."[25]

After winning the Grand Slam, Jones retired from amateur golf, but he continued to promote the sport. In November 1930, he signed a contract with Warner Bros. Pictures to make a series of 12 short films depicting techniques Jones used "in playing the shots ordinarily required in playing a round of golf." Jones described the films as "purely educational in character" and designed to increase "the enjoyment of the vast number of people already interested in the game" and to create "an interest where none exists now among the many who may find enjoyment and beneficial exercise on the golf course." By reaching millions in theaters and presenting the game "in an attractive manner," Jones's instructional reels were another reason Jones can be considered a leader in transforming golf in the public's eye.[26] Wilson argues that Jones "helped popularize golf with southerners and others who had once dismissed it as an effete game for the wealthy."[27]

A final example of Jones's personal integrity influencing others is the fact that the USGA's sportsmanship award is named in his honor. Presented annually since 1955, the Bob Jones Award recognizes an individual who "demonstrates the spirit, personal character and respect for the game exhibited by Jones." The award is considered "the highest honor bestowed by the USGA."[28] It stands as a lasting testament to the influence Jones had on not just the sport of golf but how the sport is played.

Position power comes from the authority of the position held by the leader and promotes follower compliance. Personal power comes from the leader's followers and is based on their trust, admiration, and respect for the leader.[29] Bobby Jones led by personal power to transform golf in the 1920s. By not just his athletic skill but by his integrity, vision, and commitment, he was able to capture the public imagination and popularize golf as a spectator sport. Schoenecke writes, "When golfers refer to 'the genius of Bobby Jones,' the reference is to his integrity for the golf game as well as his life."[30] President Dwight Eisenhower wrote, "Those who have been fortunate enough to know [Jones] realize that his fame as a golfer is transcended by his inestimable qualities as a human being. His gift to his friends is the warmth that comes from unselfishness, superb judgment, nobility of character, unwavering loyalty to principle." Bill Fields adds, "Those who didn't know Jones personally felt as if they did."[31] By leading indirectly, by example, and by personal power, Jones demonstrated the influence of a principled leader.

Armando Galarraga and the 28-Out Perfect Game

Principle: "The umpire is in charge."[32]

Lesson: "Nobody's perfect."

On June 2, 2010, Detroit Tigers pitcher Armando Galarraga was robbed of a perfect game by a blown call by first base umpire Jim Joyce. Both men responded to the situation in exemplary fashion given the roles they were in, but as the one suffering the wrong, it was Galarraga who best exemplifies principled leadership. From the moment of the error to the present, Galarraga has demonstrated forgiveness, empathy, humor, grace, and forgiveness. The principled leadership lesson demonstrated is perhaps best captured in the title of the book that Galarraga coauthored with Joyce: *Nobody's Perfect.*

When this particular game began, few observers would have anticipated the drama that lay in store. The visiting Cleveland Indians were in the midst of a rebuilding year, and the hometown Tigers were in a slump of their own. Just 17,738 tickets were sold for what would likely be a rather routine game.

Certainly, few spectators came expecting to see Galarraga pitch a perfect game. After a good rookie season in 2008, his performance had been mixed. In fact, he had started 2010 in the minors. Called back up in mid–May, Galarraga had just returned to the starting rotation when the Tigers traded Dontrelle Willis to Arizona on June 1.

That night, however, Galarraga was on fire. Sixty-seven of his first 88 pitches were strikes. Catcher Alex Avila recalled that Galarraga's fastball was "probably the best I had ever seen it, locating really well." Most of the outs came easily, with the exception of a great over-the-shoulder catch made by rookie center-fielder Austin Jackson in the ninth inning that robbed Mark Grudzielanek of a hit. The next batter, Mike Redmond, grounded out to the shortstop. That brought up rookie Jason Donald, who had only been called up on May 18, 2010, to replace injured shortstop Asdrubal Cabrera and was playing in just his 15th major league game. Donald had caused Galarraga trouble earlier in the game, hitting a line drive that flared just outside the right field foul line in the third inning and then hitting a deep liner to right field that was caught by Magglio Ordóñez in the sixth.[33]

This time at bat, Galarraga worked Donald to a one-ball, one-strike count. Donald swung at the next pitch and hit a slow roller in between first and second base. First baseman Miguel Cabrera used his good range to field the ball with his backhand while Galarraga raced to cover first base. Cabrera made the throw, and Galarraga caught it and then stepped on the base. Galarraga raised his arms in victory and Tigers play-by-play announcer Mario Impemba declared, "He's out!" Seconds later, Impemba said, "No! He's safe," as umpire Jim Joyce made the call.[34]

Joyce had been a major league umpire since 1987 and, according to sportswriter Tony Paul, was "considered then and now to be among the best, if not the best, at his craft." Joyce showed little hesitation in making the call, but others had immediate doubts. Among those was Galarraga, but he kept his emotions in check. Instead, he offered what Paul describes as "the most amazing reaction. He didn't swear, he didn't say a word in fact. He simply smiled—perhaps the only one in the ballpark who did."

Manager Jim Leyland walked out to first base and had a brief conversation with Joyce about the call. Cabrera was more adamant, telling Joyce, "He was out f***ing out. He was out," and continuing to press his case even after play resumed. As for Galarraga, he went back to work, and a few pitches later Trevor Crowe grounded out to third base to end the game.

Then the replay of Donald's at-bat was shown to the stadium, and the crowd erupted with a thunderous chorus of boos. Several Tiger players, including Gerald Laird and Jeremy Bonderman, unleashed their wrath on Joyce with Leyland close behind them. Joyce manfully and quietly absorbed the onslaught. He offered no defense. Later he recalled, "I started walking off the field after the 28th out. I knew then."

Amid the uproar, Galarraga remained calm and composed. He shook hands with his teammates and received a hug and some whispered words from his catcher, Avila, who said, "I just told him I was proud of him. Battling back and forth for that rotation spot, we all knew how hard he was working. I just told him I was proud of him, a great game, and that he did it."

When Joyce arrived in the umpires' locker room, the Tigers' clubhouse manager had a television cued up ready to show the replay. Joyce got to take a closer look, and there was no escaping it. He had blown the call. Paul describes Joyce as being reduced to "an emotional wreck." It would have been easy to understand if he had wanted to be left alone, but there were dozens of reporters clamoring to talk to him. Major League Baseball protocols specified a single media representative would meet with umpires to represent the pool, but rather than insisting on this limitation, Joyce told crew chief Derryl Cousins to "let them in."[35]

Joyce immediately took responsibility for his error, telling the reporters, "I kicked the sh** out of it. And I took a perfect game away from that kid who worked his a** off all night." Paul describes Joyce's sincerity, candor, and remorse as "the first step in the healing process." But, Paul adds, "the real story, for all intents and purposes, was just beginning.... A storm was coming—and a savior."[36] Now it was Galarraga's time to shine.

The Tigers watched the replay in disbelief. Galarraga watched too, and even as he did, he remained as composed as he was immediately after the call. Paul notes that at this point, Galarraga made the transition from principled man to principled leader. "The rest of the Tigers took their cue for him," Paul explains. "If he's not throwing a fit, then we can't either."[37] Thomas Boswell of the *Washington Post* described it as "a kind of cascade effect [where] one person saw unexpected virtue in another and decided, 'Well, I guess I can suck it up and do the right thing, too, if he can.'"[38] Susan Tish of the *Christian Science Monitor* adds, "The grace and dignity that Galarraga showed right from the start set the tone for everything that followed, a perfect execution of the golden rule. His sincere graciousness defused pride, stilled anger, and ultimately led us to marvel at the beauty of this moment rather than scream at its injustice."[39]

While the team proceeded to shower Galarraga with beers, Leyland went to visit Joyce, offering him a beer and a cigarette. Joyce took the cigarette. The pair was soon joined by Jeff Jones, the Tigers' bullpen coach and a former teammate of Joyce's at Bowling Green. Then came the Tigers' general manager, Dave Dombrowski. Joyce asked Dombrowski if he could speak with Galarraga, and Galarraga was immediately receptive.[40]

Speaking in the Venezuelan's native Spanish, Joyce said, "*Lo siento*" (I'm sorry). He could not muster much more, explaining later that "I couldn't talk." Galarraga simply patted Joyce on the back, noting later, "I see him completely destroyed. He feels really bad." After the brief encounter, Joyce made the lonely 45-minute drive to his mother's house in Toledo, Ohio, where he stayed when he umpired games in Detroit. He was unable to sleep that night, instead pacing the floors and smoking cigarettes. In the meantime, Galarraga went with his wife to the local Sonic, where they quietly ate their meals in the parking lot.[41]

The next day was the series' final game, and Joyce was scheduled to be the highly visible behind-the-plate umpire. Those who expected fireworks were to be disappointed. Instead, Paul writes, "there was just forgiveness and empathy." That was the way Leyland wanted the Tigers to behave, and he consulted with his longtime friend and coach Gene Lamont about how best to continue to defuse the situation. Lamont suggested Galarraga take the lineup card to Joyce. Galarraga agreed, and as soon as Joyce emerged from the tunnel behind home plate, Galarraga was on his way from the dugout. It was a moment "cited over and over through the years as a prime example of sportsmanship, of goodwill, of humanity." Joyce received the card in tears and gave Galarraga a heartfelt pat on the back. Joyce was too overcome to speak.[42]

Joyce continued to umpire until retiring prior to the 2017 season, but the blown call was always on his mind. He confesses that "I had to struggle with it every day. The ballpark reminded me of it, my job reminded me of it." The year 2010 was Galarraga's last full season in the majors, although he did not fully retire until 2015. Both men regularly give interviews about that fateful day. Their lives have also become rapidly intertwined. Just a month after the game, they appeared together in Los Angeles to present the Excellence in Sports Performance Yearly Award for the "Best Moment," and in 2011 they coauthored *Nobody's Perfect*.[43]

Principles are truths. Because of that, Galarraga was able to realize that Joyce's erroneous call "does not matter" and that "nothing can change the truth of this perfect, perfect game." Rather than complaining, Galarraga felt "the only thing for me to do is feel proud of the work I have already done, and worry about the next batter, and remember my many blessings."[44] Like Eric Liddell, Galarraga was liberated by principles that transcended lesser things, including the fact that "nobody's perfect."

Rachael Denhollander and Helping Others Find Their Voice

Principle: "How much is a little girl worth? … 'Everything' is what these survivors are worth."[45]

Lesson: When leading by example, principled leaders model principles in a way that helps others find their voice about the principles.

On September 12, 2016, the *IndyStar* reported that two former gymnasts had accused Larry Nassar, the longtime team physician for USA Gymnastics and professor in Michigan State University's Department of Family and Community Medicine, of sexual abuse. One of the accusers was Rachael Denhollander who alleged that Nassar had sexually assaulted her when she was receiving treatment for lower back pain as a 15-year-old club-level gymnast in 2000. A flood of similar accusations followed, which Nassar initially denied. Then on July 11, 2017, he pleaded guilty to child pornography and tampering with evidence charges and was sentenced to 60 years in federal prison on December 7. On January 24, 2018, Nassar was back in court, this time appearing before Judge Rosemarie Aquilina, after pleading guilty to seven counts of sexual assault of minors. Denhollander was the last of more than 150 women and girls to confront Nassar in court that day. In her victim impact statement, Denhollander posed the question, "How much is a little girl worth?" She answered with the principle that "'everything' is what these survivors are worth."

Two weeks before the article appeared in the *IndyStar*, Denhollander had filed a report with the Michigan State University Police Department and a Title IX complaint with the school alleging that Nassar had sexually assaulted her 16 years earlier when she had been his patient. Denhollander reported that Nassar gradually became more abusive over five treatments, massaging her genitals, penetrating her vagina and anus with his finger and thumb, and unhooking her bra and massaging her breasts. She said her mother was present during Nassar's treatments, but he purposely positioned himself and her in such a way that only her head and back were visible. At least seven other young women had told someone of abuse by Nassar over a 20-year period before Denhollander did, but it was Denhollander's report that finally resulted in action. Ultimately, more than 265 women would come forward alleging abuse by Nassar.

The abuse Denhollander suffered could have understandably led her to rely on raw anger and emotion when addressing Judge Aquilina, but instead Denhollander, who holds a juris doctorate from Oak Brook College of Law, based her impact statement on carefully and thoughtfully expressed logic and principle. She began by explaining that "the pursuit of justice and the protection of the innocent" are the "two major purposes in our criminal justice system." But justice and protection are values, not principles. As explained in the process identified in the Introduction, Denhollander next had to use those values to identify the principle that would serve as the framework for a systematic means of considering, deciding, communicating, measuring, and assessing her leadership actions.[46] "I realize you have many factors to consider when you fashion your sentence," she told Aquilina, "but I submit to you that the pre-eminent question in this case as you reach a decision about how best to satisfy the dual aims of this court is the same question that I asked [U.S. District] Judge [Janet] Neff to consider: 'How much is a little girl worth? How much is a young woman worth?'" The answer to these questions would be the principle that Denhollander wanted Aquilina to apply.

In expressing her answer, Denhollander first addressed the justice system's purpose of protecting the innocent. She did this by chronicling what exactly it was that these innocent ones would be protected from. Nassar, she said, "is a hardened and determined sexual predator" who "under the guise of medical treatment" subjected her to "grooming and carefully calculated brazen sexual assault [that] was the result of deliberate, premeditated, intentional and methodological patterns of abuse—patterns that were rehearsed long before I walked through Larry's exam room door and which continue to be perpetrated I believe on a daily basis for 16 more years, until I filed the police report." Then Denhollander moved beyond Nassar, reminding Aquilina that "he is not the only predator out there." By adding to the sentence already imposed on Nassar in federal court, Denhollander told Aquilina that she had the opportunity to "send a message about how seriously abuse will be taken."

Before stating the principle she wished the judge to apply in protecting the innocent, Denhollander returned to her question. "So," she asked, "how much is a little girl worth? How much priority should be placed on communicating that the fullest weight of the law will be used to protect another innocent child from the soul shattering devastation that sexual assault brings?" "I submit to you," Denhollander answered, "that these children are worth everything. Worth every protection the law can offer." For Denhollander, applying this principle meant the protection of these innocent ones was "worth the maximum sentence." That was the decision she argued Aquilina must take based on this principle.

Next, Denhollander proceeded to apply the principle in the context of pursuing justice. She explained that in this case, the court was not considering future innocents but "victims that have already been harmed ... real women and children, real women and little girls who have names and faces and souls. Real women and children whose abuse and suffering was enjoyed for sexual fulfillment by the defendant." Denhollander told Aquilina that the abuse these victims suffered "demands justice and the sentence you impose today will send a message about how much these precious women and children are worth." Justice for these victims, Denhollander concluded, "can only be realized by imposing the maximum sentence under the plea agreement."

Denhollander also used principles in directly shaming Nassar. Values, remember, are subject and personal. All organizations and individuals, even criminal, hateful, and selfish ones like Nassar, have some type of behavior that they value and embrace.[47] Nassar did what he did, Denhollander explained, because he "enjoyed it. [He] sought out and took pleasure in little girls and women being sexually injured and violated because he liked it." That was what Nassar valued.

In contrast, Denhollander explained that "throughout this process I have clung to a quote by C.S. Lewis, where he says 'My argument against God was that the universe seemed so cruel and unjust. But how had I got this idea of just and unjust? A man does not call a line crooked unless he has some idea of a straight line. What was I comparing this universe with when I called it unjust?'" It is those straight lines that are principles, and it is by that measurement that Denhollander knew the truth.

"Larry," Denhollander lectured, "I can call what you did evil and wicked—the crooked line—because it was. But I can KNOW that it was evil and wicked, because there is true goodness—the straight line against which all is measured. This straight line is not measured based on your perception of good, or mine, or any other person's. This means that I can speak the truth about my abuse, and call it what it was, in all its evil, without minimizing or mitigating, because the straight line of truth exists. And where there is true goodness, there is hope."

Denhollander's hope was not misplaced. Judge Aquilina sentenced Nassar to an additional 40–175 years in Michigan State prison. On February 5, 2018, Nassar was sentenced to 40–125 more years after pleading guilty to an additional three counts of sexual assault. He will most certainly remain in prison until he dies.

Denhollander's eloquent imagery of a "straight line of truth" that is measured not by subjective and personal interpretation but by objective and universal principle wonderfully captures the clarity associated with principled decision-making. Her impact statement received a standing ovation and prompted Judge Aquilina to call her "the bravest person I've ever had in my courtroom." But Denhollander went beyond mere personal adherence to principle and became a principled leader. Aquilina told Denhollander, "You built an army of survivors" and called her "a five-star general." "You started the tidal wave," Aquilina continued. "You made all of this happen. You made all of these voices matter."

Denhollander did so by leading by example. Leading by example goes beyond merely doing what is supposed to be done. Every person of principle should be doing that. Leading by example is a way a leader influences others by using himself or herself to elicit a desired behavior response. Good leadership by example elicits something from followers and helps them understand something about themselves.[48] To that extent, leadership experts such as James Kouzes, Barry Posner, and Stephen Covey connect leading by example with "finding one's voice." This means that the leader finds his or her voice and then helps others find theirs.[49] By telling her story with boldness, persistence, passion, and clarity, Denhollander inspired others to do so as well.

Literary Characters

Atticus Finch and Empathy

Principle: "You never really understand a person until you consider things from his point of view—until you climb into his skin and walk around in it."[1]

Lesson: Principled leadership should be worthy of emulation.

To Kill a Mockingbird is a novel by Harper Lee published in 1960 that takes place in the 1930s in the fictional town of Maycomb, Alabama. A local Black man named Tom Robinson is falsely accused of raping a white woman named Mayella Ewell. Atticus Finch is the lawyer appointed by Judge John Taylor to defend Tom, and throughout the trial Atticus displays remarkable empathy, not just for Tom but for Mayella as well. The novel is narrated by Atticus's daughter, six-year-old Jean Louise, nicknamed "Scout," who grows to emulate her father's empathy in her relationship with her reclusive neighbor Arthur "Boo" Radley.

An early encounter with empathy occurs when Scout's teacher, Miss Caroline Fisher, a new arrival to Maycomb, offers to loan lunch money to Scout's classmate Walter Cunningham. Walter declines Miss Caroline's generosity, which causes her to become increasingly impatient because she cannot understand what she considers to be Walter's irrationality. Scout intervenes and explains to Miss Caroline that Walter did not forget his lunch; his family is simply too poor to provide him one. Furthermore, Scout tells Miss Caroline, "The Cunninghams never took anything they can't pay back—no church baskets and no scrip stamps. They never took anything off of anybody, they get along on what they have. They don't have much, but they get along on it."[2] By insisting on trying to loan Walter money, Scout tells

Miss Caroline, "you're shaming him.... Walter hasn't got a quarter to bring you." Scout's well-intentioned attempts to make Miss Caroline understand only exasperate her more, and Miss Caroline tells Scout, "I've had about enough of you this morning" and gives Scout a series of strikes on her hand with a ruler. When the class is dismissed for lunch, Scout sees Miss Caroline sink down in her chair and bury her head in her arms. "Had her conduct been more friendly toward me," Scout muses, "I would have felt sorry for her."[3] At this point in her development, Scout displays very little empathy for Miss Caroline.

Later that evening, Scout tells Atticus about "the day's misfortunes," including her encounter with Miss Caroline and begs him not to send her back to school. Atticus replies with a lesson on empathy, telling Scout, "First of all, if you can learn a simple trick, Scout, you'll get along a lot better with all kinds of folks. You never really understand a person until you consider things from his point of view—until you climb into his skin and walk around in it." He explains that they can't expect Miss Caroline "to learn all Maycomb's ways in one day" and that if Scout and Walter "had put ourselves in her shoes we'd have seen it was an honest mistake on her part." Atticus argues that they could not hold Miss Caroline responsible "when she knew no better."[4]

This fairly simple example of Atticus's empathy is small compared to the understanding he shows toward Mayella when it is learned that contrary to her being raped, it was actually she who made sexual advances toward Tom and that her father beat her when he found out about it. Atticus tells the jury, "I have nothing but pity in my heart for the chief witness for the state. She is the victim of cruel poverty and ignorance." Atticus explains that by kissing Tom, a Black man, Mayella broke "a rigid and time honored code of our society, a code so severe that whoever breaks it is hounded from our midst as unfit to live with." Because of that, Mayella "must destroy the evidence of her offense," and that evidence was Tom. In spite of this ability to empathize with Mayella, Atticus declares, "But my pity does not extend so far as to her putting a man's life at stake which she has done in an effort to get rid of her own guilt."[5]

Under cross-examination by prosecutor Horace Gilmer, Tom also displays empathy. When asked why he helped Mayella, Tom explains that it "looked like she didn't have nobody to help her." Even though her father and several siblings lived in the house as well, Tom said Mayella "seemed to try more'n the rest of 'em." But when Tom continues that "I felt right sorry for her," this expression of sympathy evokes the furor and disdain of Gilmer and much of the courtroom. As he bears this latest unjust burden, a chastised Tom "realized his mistake," but Atticus later comes to his defense and chides the critics for their condemnation of Tom's "unmitigated temerity to 'feel sorry' for a white woman."[6]

Additional insight into Atticus's empathy comes from the unlikely source of Dolphus Raymond, a wealthy white resident of Maycomb who has become a social outcast because of his sexual association with Black women. In a brief encounter with Scout and her friend Dill during a break in the trial, Raymond tells Scout he could easily say "the hell with" his critics, but instead he empathizes with them. Rather than forcing them to come to grips with the illogic of their sentiments, he pretends to be a drunk. Raymond knows his charade "ain't honest but it's mighty helpful to folks" in giving them something they can "latch onto" because he knows "they could never, never understand that I live like I do because that's the way I want to live."[7]

In spite of his willingness to personally absorb mistreatment, Raymond remains sensitive to injustice visited on others. He counsels Scout and Dill about "the hell white people give colored folks, without even stopping to think that they're people, too." In contrast to such cruel indifference, Raymond tells Scout that "your pa's not a run-of-the-mill man."[8]

Scout then returns to the courtroom where Raymond's soliloquy serves as an apropos precursor to Atticus's closing remarks to the jury. Atticus painstakingly and emotionally explains to the jury the Jeffersonian concept of equality and challenges them to treat Tom equally as they "review without passion the evidence you have heard." He admonishes the jury to "in the name of God, believe him," rather than the testimony of two white witnesses that has been "called into serious question." To do so, the jury will have to have the empathy to see Tom as a fellow human being, in a court where indeed "all men are created equal."[9]

In spite of Atticus's efforts, justice does not prevail, and Tom is found guilty. While Tom is in prison, he attempts to escape and is shot dead by the guards. Atticus had already been planning an appeal and had told Tom "we had such a good chance," but he does not fault Tom for trying to escape. Instead of looking at it from his perspective as a white man and a lawyer, Atticus empathizes with Tom and explains that "I guess Tom was tired of white men's chances and preferred to take his own."[10]

Although Atticus's tremendous empathy was not enough to save Tom, it does seem to have a profound effect on Scout. After the trial has ended and school has started back up, Scout is again making her regular trips past the Radley house. Now, however, she confesses that "I sometimes felt a twinge of remorse, when passing by the old place, at ever having taken part in what must have been sheer torment to Arthur Radley—what reasonable recluse wants children peeping through his shutters, delivering greetings on the end of a fishing pole, wandering in his collards at night?"[11] As Scout and her brother Jem return home late one night after a school Halloween pageant, Mayella's father, Robert E. Lee "Bob" Ewell, who has been humiliated by the truth Atticus presented during the trial, attacks them. Ewell is able to injure Jem, but Boo intervenes and kills Ewell before he can cause more harm and then carries an unconscious Jem home.

When it is discovered that Boo is the hero, it is Sheriff Heck Tate who shows great empathy, telling Atticus, who is struggling to process the situation, that "maybe you'll say it's my duty to tell the town all about it and not hush it up. Know what'd happen then? All the ladies in Maycomb includin' my wife'd be knocking on his door bringing angel food cakes. To my way of thinkin', Mr. Finch, taking the one man who's done you and this town a great service an' draggin' him with his shy ways into the limelight—to me, that's a sin. It's a sin and I'm not about to have it on my head. If it was any other man it'd be different. But not this man, Mr. Finch."[12] Atticus finally comes around to understand the necessity of Sheriff Tate's logic.

As Jem sleeps, Scout helps a cautious Boo check on him and lightly brush Jem's hair. Scout notes she "was beginning to learn [Boo's] body English. His hand tightened on mine and he indicated that he wanted to leave." At Boo's request, Scout walks him home. As she reflects on all that has happened and her new appreciation of Boo and life itself, she recalls that "Atticus was right. One time he said you never really know a man until you stand in his shoes and walk around in them. Just standing on the Radley porch was enough."[13] Back safely at home, Scout begs Atticus to read her a story of a misunderstood boy. As she drifts off to sleep, she tells Atticus the boy in the story turned out to be "real nice." "Most people are, Scout," Atticus replies, "when you finally see them."[14]

Empathy is a common theme throughout *To Kill a Mockingbird*, and it is displayed in many forms and by many characters. Perhaps it is most commonly associated with Atticus because he is the central figure that connects so many of the other demonstrations. His principle to consider things from another person's point of view is certainly not lost on Scout, who comes to model her father's empathy in her relationship with Boo.

Scout's growth is the result of many influences. Atticus teaches her empathy by explaining events such as the encounter with Miss Caroline in those terms. He certainly models empathy in his treatment of Tom, and Scout witnesses this example. Scout even receives validation of how empathy elevates Atticus from the testimony of Raymond. Finally, Scout learns from her own self-reflection as she processes her history with Boo. If General Bill Creech is correct that "the first duty of a leader is to create more leaders,"[15] then Atticus certainly did his duty to Scout. In this case, the outcome seems particularly logical because if principles are indeed universal truths, once someone is exposed to them, like Scout, they should want to make them their own and central to their leadership philosophy.

Jim and Principled Leadership Based on Personal Authority

Principle: "We do not know much about Jim, but we do know that he has great love for his family and longs for the day when he will be free in order to reclaim them. In the meantime, Huck is his family."[16]

Lesson: The practice of principled leadership is not dependent on positional authority.

One of the main themes of *The Adventures of Huckleberry Finn* is Huck's attempts to reconcile what he considers good and what society considers bad and vice versa. This struggle is most apparent in Huck's dilemma about whether to help or hinder Jim's pursuit of freedom. The degree to which Huck (as well as author Mark Twain) exhibits the characteristics of a principled leader in this regard has been the subject of much debate, and that debate will not be continued here. Instead, the focus of this study is Jim, who, in serving as a father figure to Huck, clearly acts as a principled leader, even at great sacrifice to himself. Among the main lessons taught by Jim, who is a slave and therefore below Huck in the societal hierarchy, is that the practice of principled leadership is not dependent on positional authority.

Huck's natural father, "Pap," certainly is no role model. He comes and goes, beats Huck for going to school, and once locked Huck alone in the cabin for three days. Huck describes Pap's routine as "every time he got money he got drunk; and every time he got drunk he raised Cain around town; and every time he raised Cain he got jailed."[17] He would also beat Huck until he "was all over welts."[18] When Huck can take it no more, he runs away, leaving behind an elaborate scene that gives the impression he has been murdered by robbers.

Huck steals away in a canoe he had found earlier and makes his way to Jackson's Island. He soon discovers someone else is on the island, and with some trepidation he sets out to find out who it is. To his relief, it is Jim, whom he knows as a slave belonging to Miss Watson, the stern, severe sister of the widow Douglas and who has joined her sister in trying to "sivilize" Huck.[19] After Jim and Huck talk for a while, Huck asks Jim, "How do you come to be here, Jim, and how'd you get here?" After getting Huck to promise he won't tell, Jim confesses that he has "run off" to avoid what he thinks is Miss Watson's intent "to sell me down to Orleans." Huck immediately recognizes the dilemma he is now in between being loyal to his word not to betray Jim and the expectations of society. Huck vows to keep his promise even though "people will call me a low-down Abolitionist and despise me for keeping mum."[20]

Almost immediately, Jim assumes the role as Huck's protector. When a two-story frame house floats by, Jim and Huck see "something laying on the floor that looked like a man." Jim goes to investigate and discovers a dead man who has been shot in the back. The man is naked and appears to have been dead for two or three days. Jim tells Huck "doan' look at his face—it's too gashly."[21] Not only does Jim protect Huck from the gruesome sight; he protects Huck from the knowledge that the dead man is Pap. It is not until the last page of the book when all are safe that Jim tells Huck he can go retrieve his money without fear because the dead man in the house was Pap.[22]

One of the most basic roles of a father is to provide shelter. Pap never provided Huck a safe place to live, but Jim quickly transforms the raft from an uncomfortable and dangerous place fully exposed to the elements and the waves of passing steamboats into what Huck declares a "snug wigwam." Jim does this by building a floor a foot or so above the level of the raft and leaning several planks against each other to make the enclosed area. Now the travelers "have a place to get under in blazing weather and to keep the things dry."[23] With Pap, Huck had lived in a barrel and a run-down cabin. With Jim, Huck learns "there warn't no home like a raft."[24] As the pair float along, Betty Jones says they do so as "mentor and student, father and son."[25]

Jim's care for Huck manifests itself in many other ways. The two take shifts staying awake and keeping a lookout on the raft, but Jim often pulls Huck's shift for him and lets him sleep. Jim lovingly calls Huck "honey." In short, in Jim, Huck has someone who would "do everything he could think of for me" and who was "good ... always" to Huck.[26]

In spite of Jim's care for Huck, Huck only gradually evolves into a full appreciation of not just Jim's humanity but Jim's importance to him. In the aptly titled chapter "Fooling Poor Old Jim," Huck plays a mean and juvenile trick on Jim. The pair get separated in a dense fog, and although Huck is "sick and scared"[27] with anxiety, once the danger passes he tries to convince Jim that the fog was just a dream. This is after Jim has expressed heartfelt joy that Huck is alive after fearing he had drowned. "It's too good for true, honey, it's too good for true," cries Jim only for Huck to cruelly respond, "What's the matter with you, Jim? You been a-drinking?"[28] Once Jim figures out Huck has made up the story, Jim assumes the fatherly role of teacher and admonisher.

> When I got all wore out wid work, en wid de callin' for you, en went to sleep, my heart wuz mos' broke bekase you wuz los', en I didn' k'yer no' mo' what become er me en de raf'. En when I wake up en fine you back ag'in, all safe en soun', de tears come, en I could a got down on my knees en kiss yo' foot, I's so thankful. En all you wuz thinkin' 'bout wuz how you could make a fool uv ole Jim wid a lie. Dat truck dah is *trash*; en trash is what people is dat puts dirt on de head er dey fren's en makes 'em ashamed.[29]

A chastened and humbled Huck learns his lesson and comes to see Jim in a new way as a fellow human being with feelings.[30]

This incremental growth is an example of how Jim fulfills his role as mentor to "guide Huck into the light while taking care that the journey is made gradually, in stages that prepare the initiate's consciousness." While Jim may fully understand the principles at stake, he is astutely aware of the developmental stage Huck is in. His role is "to ask the right questions of Huck, to provide him with situations that offer potential for knowledge, and to act always as a stable and consistent force of morality for him."[31]

As part of this process, Jim also exposes Huck to how a real father cares for his children, displaying what Jocelyn Chadwick-Joshua lauds as Jim's "indomitable faith in the nuclear family (a faith that extends into Huckleberry Finn)."[32] With great thoughtfulness and passion, Jim describes for Huck his plan to save up enough money to buy his wife out of slavery and then for the two of them to work together to buy their two children. Jim is so adamant about rescuing his children he tells Huck that "if their master wouldn't sell them, they'd get an Ab'litionist to go and steal them." When Huck first hears such talk of stealing slaves, it "froze" him because of its violation of the norms of Huck's society.[33] Almost immediately, though, when Jim declares Huck to be "de bes' fren' Jim's ever had; en you's de *only* fren' ole Jim's got now," Huck experiences more growth in his understanding and appreciation of Jim, and Huck subsequently lies to protect Jim from some fugitive slave hunters.[34]

Ultimately, Jim decides to risk his own freedom to help secure a doctor to care for the wounded Tom Sawyer. After Huck and Jim have been "consulting—and thinking" about how to handle this situation, Huck asks Jim to say what he has concluded. In a beautiful testimony to empathy and loyalty, Jim describes how he has imagined a role reversal where it is Tom "dat 'uz bein' sot free, en one er de boys wuz to git shot" and in need of a doctor. Jim believes that Tom would sacrifice his freedom to save someone else, and Jim resolves to do the same. The callousness of Huck's racist comment that he now "knowed [Jim] was white inside" does not erase the valuable lesson Jim has taught Huck about sacrifice and loyalty.[35] Huck's appreciation of Jim's act of selflessness is confirmed by the doctor's testimony that "I never see a nigger that was a better nuss or faithfuler, and yet he was risking his freedom to do it."[36] In contrast to all the craven selfishness Huck has seen in Pap and other adults, Jim has demonstrated in a very profound way what it is to put others first.

This and the other moral development Huck experiences "could not take place without the ever-present stimulus and challenge provided by his friendship with Jim." Because of this relationship, Betty Jones declares Jim to be "a moral *necessity*" for Huck.[37] In similar fashion, Kenny Williams argues, "Whenever Huck is inclined to let the baseness of his human condition assume control, it is Jim who guides him. The bond between the two characters is so strong that if one takes Jim away, Huck—as we know him—ceases to exist."[38] As instructor, role model, redeemer, and conscience to Huck, it is Jim who elevates Huck from the previous limitations placed on him by Pap and society. The future is now boundless for Huck, and his past no longer holds him back. As the story ends, Huck tells the reader, "I reckon I got to light out for the territory ahead of the rest."[39] Jim is now free, and Huck is too. That a slave could liberate a white boy is a testimony to Jim's character and leadership. By relying on personal authority rather than positional authority, Jim demonstrates principled leadership's emphasis on "commitment" rather than "compliance."

Jiggs Casey and Civilian Control of the Military

Principle: Civilian control of the military
Lesson: Principles help people navigate divided loyalties.

Seven Days in May is a work of fiction about a planned coup orchestrated by Chairman of the Joint Chiefs of Staff General James Mattoon Scott in response to President Jordan Lyman's negotiations of a nuclear disarmament treaty with the Soviet Union. A key figure in uncovering and thwarting the cabal is "Jiggs" Casey, a Marine Corps colonel who serves under Scott as the director of the Joint Chiefs of Staff. Although Casey shares Scott's reservations about the treaty, Casey's adherence to the principle of civilian control of the military prevents him from seeing a coup as an option.

Samuel Huntington explored the idea of civilian control of the military in 1959 in his seminal *The Soldier and the State.* Huntington identified three responsibilities of military men to the state. These were to represent the claims of military security within the state machine, to offer advice on alternative courses of action from a military point of view, and "to implement state decisions with respect to military security even if it is a decision which runs violently counter to his military judgment."[40] In all cases, Huntington argued that "the superior political wisdom of the statesman must be accepted as a fact" and "that the military are the servants of the statesman, and that civilian control is essential to military professionalism."[41] He advocated "objective" civilian control, which is based on the "maximizing of military professionalism" and which "renders the military politically sterile and neutral."[42] Casey appears to be Huntington's type of professional, declaring that "as a military officer, I stand clear of politics."

Fletcher Knebel and Charles Bailey published *Seven Days in May* as a book in 1961, and it was made into a movie in 1964. Set in the midst of the Cold War, *Seven Days in May* resonates with the international tension and political drama of the time. The threat of Soviet aggression and the potential for a world war necessitated that the United States maintain a strong military arsenal, but the presence of such a massive force was itself a danger. In his Farewell Address to the

Nation on January 17, 1961, President Dwight Eisenhower acknowledged that in order to keep the peace, "our arms must be mighty, ready for instant action, so that no potential aggressor may be tempted to risk his own destruction." Yet Eisenhower also noted that the "conjunction of an immense military establishment and a large arms industry is new in the American experience" and the country "must not fail to comprehend its grave implications." He cautioned that "we must guard against the acquisition of unwarranted influence, whether sought or unsought, by the military-industrial complex. The potential for the disastrous rise of misplaced power exists, and will persist."[43] Gerald Pratley writes, "*Seven Days in May* was the opportunity to illustrate what a tremendous force the military-industrial complex is."[44]

Whereas Eisenhower's status as a five-star general and the supreme commander of the Allied Expeditionary Force in Europe during World War II solidified his military credentials, his successor, John F. Kennedy, was more susceptible to Cold War criticism, especially after the disastrous Bay of Pigs invasion failed to oust Fidel Castro from Cuba in 1961. Indeed, Scott's character in *Seven Days in May* is commonly considered to have been inspired by two of Kennedy's key military advisers who often sparred with their chief.[45]

The first was the intensely anti–Communist Major General Edwin Walker who was commander of the 24th Infantry Division in Augsburg, Germany. In April 1961, Walker was accused of indoctrinating his troops with right-wing literature from the John Birch Society. With the agreement of Kennedy, Secretary of Defense Robert McNamara relieved Walker of his command and initiated an investigation. Walker resigned in protest, and his followers used the affair as an opportunity to accuse the Kennedy administration of trying to muzzle anti–Communist military officers.

A second inspiration for Scott was the bombastic air force chief of staff Curtis LeMay whom Robert Dalleck describes as a "burly, cigar-chomping caricature of a general [who] believed the United States had no choice but to bomb its foes into submission." Dismissive of civilian control of the decision-making process, LeMay complained of an American phobia about nuclear weapons and was prepared to launch a preemptive nuclear first strike against the Soviet Union. During the Cuban missile crisis, he forcefully opposed anything short of direct military action. Theodore Sorensen, Kennedy's speechwriter and alter ego, considered LeMay to be "my least favorite human being."[46]

Scott is an imposing character who earned six Purple Hearts, two Distinguished Service Crosses, and the Medal of Honor as an air force fighter pilot. His plan is to execute the coup under the cover of a training exercise. A secret army unit known as ECOMCON (Emergency Communications Control) will take control of the country's communications networks and seize Lyman, who believes he is participating in a staged "alert." Scott will then become the head of the military junta.

Scott is not alone in his objection to Lyman's treaty. The U.S. public also has its doubts, and the president's popularity has dropped to 29 percent. Riots break out in front of the White House, and the military is especially dissatisfied with the treaty. To prepare the public to receive him, Scott has been participating in several nationally televised rallies protesting the treaty. To make matters worse for Lyman, he is diagnosed with a dangerous heart condition but feels too consumed by the national unrest to take the two-week vacation the doctor orders.

As the film's title suggests, Casey stumbles on Scott's plan just seven days before the coup is scheduled to be initiated. Even though he also opposes Scott's policies, Casey cannot tolerate a coup and reports the plan to Lyman. As the two men discuss the situation, in spite of whatever other reservations he may have, the principle of civilian control of the military emerges as the defining aspect of Casey's thought process:

> LYMAN: I know what Scott's attitude on the treaty is. What's yours?
>
> CASEY: I agree with General Scott, sir. I think we're being played for suckers. I think it's really your business. Yours and the Senate. You did it, and they agreed so, well, I don't see how we in the military can question it. I mean we can question it, but we can't fight it. We shouldn't anyway.
>
> LYMAN: Jiggs, isn't it? Isn't that what they call you?
>
> CASEY: Yes, sir.
>
> LYMAN: So you, uh, you stand by the Constitution, Jiggs?

CASEY: I never thought of it just like that, Mr. President, but, well, that's what we got and I guess it's worked pretty well so far. I sure don't want to be the one to say we ought to change it.

LYMAN: Neither do I.

Lyman then gathers a small group of trusted advisers to investigate the situation and uses a fishing trip as an excuse not to participate in Scott's alert. Lyman gives Casey the unsavory task of using his romantic chemistry with Eleanor Holbrook, a Washington socialite who was Scott's former mistress, to gather details of Scott's private life that may give Lyman leverage. Casey accomplishes the mission but takes no pleasure in it. He reports the information to Secretary of the Treasury Christopher Todd who declares it "dynamite" and tells Casey, "Any taste of victory we have in our mouths, Colonel, is due in no small measure to your efforts." The ensuing exchange indicates the struggle Casey is experiencing:

CASEY: The taste I've got in my mouth, Mr. Secretary, is unmentionable.

TODD: I can understand that feeling, Colonel. But when you deal with a jackal like your general…

CASEY: Mr. Todd, this is a full air force general. Six times wounded, wearing only half the medals he deserves. Whatever else he is, he's no jackal.

Even Lyman understands the complexities of the issue. When Lyman announces his plan to summon Scott to his office, Todd gleefully seconds, "I think it's time we faced the enemy, Mr. President." Lyman retorts,

> He's not the enemy. Scott, the Joint Chiefs, even the very emotional, very illogical lunatic fringe—they're not the enemy. The enemy's an age—a nuclear age. It happens to have killed man's faith in his ability to influence what happens to him. And out of this comes a sickness, and out of sickness a frustration, a feeling of impotence, helplessness, weakness. And from this, this desperation, we look for a champion in red, white, and blue. Every now and then a man on a white horse rides by, and we appoint him to be our personal god for the duration. For some men it was a Senator McCarthy, for others it was a General Walker, and now it's a General Scott.

Lyman confronts Scott with the evidence and demands that he and his coconspirators resign. Scott denies the existence of any coup plot, refuses to resign, and instead lambasts Lyman and the treaty.

When Scott claims to be motivated only by "an abiding interest in the survival of this country" and that the American people are behind him, Lyman challenges him to resign and run for office through the legitimate democratic process. With Scott still defiant, Lyman considers confronting him with the damning letters from Holbrook but instead decides not to resort to such a tactic.

An unrepentant Scott leaves Lyman and meets with the other three joint chiefs, reasserting his intention to go through with the coup. Even when a handwritten confession extracted from Vice Admiral Farley Barnswell by Lyman's longtime adviser Paul Girard surfaces and makes knowledge of the plot public, Scott is undeterred. Only when the three other joint chiefs tender their resignations does Scott abandon his plan.

The film ends with Lyman making a moving oration in a televised press conference in which he champions the values of America. Posing a sharp contrast with the intrigues of men like Scott, Lyman tells America,

> There's been abroad in this land in recent months a whisper that we have somehow lost our greatness, that we do not have the strength to win without war the struggles for liberty throughout the world. This is slander because our country is strong, strong enough to be a peacemaker. It is proud, proud enough to be patient. The whisperers and the detractors, the violent men are wrong. We will remain strong and proud, peaceful and patient, and we will see a day when on this earth all men will walk out of the long tunnels of tyranny into the bright sunshine of freedom.

Lyman exits the scene to a standing ovation from the reporters. In contrast, Scott departs in his car, being driven away, defeated and without fanfare. Clearly, *Seven Days in May* is a celebration of civilian control of the military and the Constitution.

Seven Days in May was one of several films in the 1960s that posed a stark contrast between "real patriots" such as Jiggs Casey and "fanatics, true believers, and self-styled super-patriots" such as James Mattoon Scott. Michael Coyne writes that the films typically featured "decent men ... faced with difficult, often cruel choices." In such situations, principles guided the heroes through a web of divided loyalties, and it is well they did because, Coyne continues, "the Republic is dependent on such men."[47]

Juror Number 8 and a Fair Trial

Principle: Innocent until proven guilty.

Lesson: Principled leaders "lift people out of their petty preoccupations and unite them toward higher ends."[48]

12 Angry Men, a 1957 film written by Reginald Rose, tells the story of a jury deliberating the trial of an 18-year-old boy accused of murdering his father. A unanimous vote is required for a guilty verdict, and in the initial vote, all members except "Juror Number 8," played by Henry Fonda, vote guilty. At this point, Juror Number 8 is not convinced that the accused boy is not guilty, only that more discussion is necessary before the notion of reasonable doubt can adequately be addressed. His commitment to the principle that accused people are innocent until proven guilty sustains him in overcoming a host of obstacles, including the "petty preoccupations" that distract his fellow jurors.

Fonda's character is under intense pressure from several of the other jurors to change his vote. His main antagonist is Juror Number 3, a father who viewers learn later is in part motivated by his difficulties with his own son. Juror Number 7 appears more interested in getting to the Yankees baseball game than deciding the fate of the boy's life. Juror Number 10 is influenced by his negative opinion of immigrants. The foreman, who by position should be the leader of the group, takes a passive approach to his duties. By a combination of logic, patience, cunning, and persuasion, Juror Number 8 convinces his fellow jurors to one by one change their votes.

In helping his fellow jurors transcend their distractions and biases, Juror Number 8 is fulfilling John Gardner's challenge for leaders to "conceive and articulate goals in ways that lift people out of their petty preoccupations and unite them toward higher ends." This transformation can occur when a leader revitalizes a group's commitment to its values. Gardner explains that leaders "keep the values fresh" so that they can become "sources of motivation for the exertions required of the group."[49]

The Sixth Amendment to the Constitution of the United States accords the accused "the right to a speedy and public trial, by an impartial jury." In providing this constitutional right, jurors have tremendous power and responsibility. They have the power to determine whether a person is guilty or not guilty. They have the responsibility to wield that power with fairness, impartiality, and care. Colloquially, jurors are summoned to jury "duty," and jury service is often described by such phrases as "a high duty of citizenship" and "the most valuable duty a citizen can perform in peacetime." In keeping with this idea of duty, the judge in *12 Angry Men* advises the jurors that "it now becomes your duty to try and separate the facts from the fancy." "One man is dead. The life of another is at stake," the judge says. "I urge you to deliberate honestly and thoughtfully. If this is a reasonable doubt—then you must bring me a verdict of 'not guilty.'" These instructions frame the principle that guides Juror Number 8.

There is much ambiguity and subjectivity in the evidence presented at the trial that does in fact create reasonable doubt. Did noise from a passing train make it impossible to hear what one witness claims to have heard? Did the accused literally mean it when he said, "I'm going to kill you"? Could a witness really have made it to his front door in the short time he claimed to have? Was a woman not wearing her glasses and therefore unable to clearly see what she testified that she did? Did the angle of the stab wound make sense? Nonetheless, "petty preoccupations" plague each juror's ability to weigh the evidence in the context of their civic duty and the judge's instructions.

Yet Juror Number 8 persists. As he explores the implications of the case's uncertainties, one by one the other jurors change their votes. Finally, only Juror Number 3 clings to his guilty vote, but the process has increasingly forced him to come to grips with the impact of his strained relationship with his own son and his transference of that situation to the present one. His struggle reaches a climax as he tears up a picture of his son and him and then breaks down in a fit of sobs. Released from that burden, he mutters, "not guilty," making the jury unanimous.

Juror Number 8 took seriously the judge's admonition to deliberate honestly and thoughtfully. One challenge facing him, however, was that not all of his fellow jurors valued this duty and the power and responsibility it entailed. Juror Number 8 never advocates guilt or innocence or argues one way or another that the accused had or had not committed the murder. What he does do is to resolutely pursue a path of systematic inquiry and critical thinking about the facts of the case. He only seeks to explore those areas of reasonable doubt. This exploration requires time, and he steadfastly reminds his fellow jurors the "higher end" that is at stake and its priority over their "petty preoccupations." "This is somebody's life," he tells them. "We can't decide in five minutes." When he sees two jurors playing tic-tac-toe rather than listening to the discussion, he crumples up their paper and declares, "This isn't a game." Juror Number 3 responds by protesting Juror Number 8's "absolute nerve" and asking, "Who does he think he is?" Juror Number 8 is able to withstand this and other personal attacks because of his laser-like focus on principle. As a testimony to Juror Number 8's ability to transcend personality, he helps the distraught Juror Number 3—his greatest nemesis and a man who once physically threatened him—with his coat as the jurors depart. Juror Number 8 does not see the trial's outcome as a victory over Juror Number 3. He sees it as a victory for justice.

Another challenge facing Juror Number 8 is that the entire jury is subject to the effects of groupthink. Research psychologist Irving Janis describes groupthink as "a mode of thinking that people engage in when they are deeply involved in a cohesive in-group, when the members' strivings for unanimity override their motivation to realistically appraise alternative courses of action."[50] It is "the tendency for groups to reach decisions without accurately assessing their consequences, because individual members tend to go along with ideas they think the others support."[51] This tendency is generated by the individual's preference to take the easy route and avoid being criticized and alienated for advocating a position that is contrary to that of other members. The result is "close-mindedness or a collective reluctance to question basic assumptions about the problem at hand," resulting in a "shared illusion" of consensus within the group.[52]

Janis cites seven major pitfalls that generally afflict group problem-solving. The one that most impacts this discussion of principled leadership is that "the group does not survey the objectives to be fulfilled and the values implicated by the choice."[53] Juror Number 8's fellow jurors do not seem to comprehend that their choice to pursue their duty in a casual and undisciplined way implicates that they value personal convenience and bias more than they value the life of another human being and justice.

In contrast, Juror Number 8 was resolute in his conviction that the accused deserved a fair trial and that the jury do its duty. His steadiness was not borne of stubbornness, an unwillingness to change, or narrow-mindedness. In fact, Juror Number 8 always had an open mind and was inquisitive and seeking. His steadiness was in his commitment to the principle of justice and the accused's right to a fair trial. It was that foundation that allowed him to weather all the attacks, contradictions, unknowns, and biases that would have distracted a less grounded leader. In the process, Juror Number 8 demonstrated how adherence to a principle can help a leader follow Gardner's challenge to "conceive and articulate goals in ways that lift people out of their petty preoccupations and unite them toward higher ends."[54]

Societal Leaders

Rosa Parks and the Montgomery Bus Boycott

Principle: "It was unfair to segregate us."[1]

Lesson: Principles transcend values.

According to Stephen Covey, principles transcend other factors in that even though different cultures may translate principles into different practices and the wrongful use of freedom may obscure principles over time, the principles remain. Covey equates them to natural laws that operate constantly.[2] When John Knox opened the second day of the Constitutional Convention of the state of Alabama on May 22, 1901, he declared the work ahead was to "within the limits imposed by the Federal Constitution, to establish white supremacy in this State."[3] Based on such values, a series of Jim Crow laws emerged in Alabama and throughout the South that was designed to secure white political domination and segregate the races. One such regulation was the Montgomery, Alabama, city ordinance that required Black passengers to sit in the back half of city buses and to relinquish their seats to white riders if the white section in the front of the bus was full. In a historic show of "principled defiance,"[4] Rosa Parks refused to obey this law on December 1, 1955, demonstrating Covey's supremacy of principles to other factors.

When Parks first boarded the bus that day, there were several empty seats in the white section. Parks took an aisle seat in the racially neutral middle section, behind the movable "colored" sign. There, she joined a Black man sitting next to her on the window side, and there were two Black women sitting across the aisle. At the next two stops, enough white passengers boarded to nearly fill the white section, and at the third stop, the last white seats were taken and one white man was left standing. Because no Black person was allowed to sit parallel to a white person, the bus driver commanded all four of the Black passengers to "move y'all, I want those two seats." At first, no one moved. When the driver reiterated that "y'all better make it light on yourselves and let me have those seats," the two Black women across the aisle got up and moved to the back of the bus. The man beside Parks got up too, and Parks swung her legs to the side to let him pass. Then she slid over to the window seat.[5]

The bus driver moved toward Parks to confront her noncompliance and demanded, "Are you going to stand up?" When Parks replied, "No," the driver said, "Well, I'm going to have you arrested." A resolute Parks softly answered, "You may do that." Two police officers soon arrived, listened to the driver's account, and then moved to Parks. Officer F.B. Day asked Parks why she had refused the driver's order, and she answered with a question: "Why do you all push us around?" Parks's biographer Douglas Brinkley records that it was "a question that had no moral answer," and whether he intended it to or not, Day's response seems to support the statement. "I don't know," he said, "but the law is the law, and you're under arrest."[6]

Word of Parks's arrest spread quickly through the Black community, and soon there was talk of making hers the test case to challenge the segregated bus ordinance. Parks was not the first Black rider to defy the ordinance. Fifteen-year-old Claudette Colvin had done the same thing nine months earlier, but the National Association for the Advancement of Colored People (NAACP) and other Black organizations did not think the time or the person was right. As Colvin recalls, "They didn't think teenagers would be reliable."[7] Parks, on the other hand, had the maturity, bearing, experience and training as an activist, and character to carry this awesome responsibility. Still, there would be incredible risks. In addition to the dangerous threats to the physical safety of herself and her family, Parks would very likely lose her job, a circumstance compounded by the fact that she was the family's principal breadwinner. Her husband would also become a target for white retaliation. Her mother was in frail health. Guardedly, Edgar Daniel (E.D.) Nixon, president of the local chapter of the NAACP, said, "Mrs. Parks, with your permission, we can break down segregation on the bus[es] with your case."[8] "If you think it will mean something to Montgomery and do some good," she replied, "I'll be happy to go along with it."[9] Brinkley notes that with those words, "an ordinary, civic-minded woman gave birth to the modern civil rights movement."[10]

Among those who saw the opportunity presented by Parks's arrest was Jo Ann Robinson of the Women's Political Council. Robinson sprang into action, and by 4:00 a.m. the day after Parks's arrest, she had tens of thousands of leaflets prepared that read:

> Another woman has been arrested and thrown in jail because she refused to get up out of her seat on the bus for a white person to sit down. It is the second time since the Claudette Colvin case that a Negro woman has been arrested for the same thing. This has to be stopped. Negroes have rights too, for if Negroes did not ride the buses, they could not operate. Three-fourths of the riders are Negro, yet we are arrested, or have to stand over empty seats. If we do not do something to stop these arrests, they will continue. The next time it may be you, or your daughter, or mother. This woman's case will come up on Monday. We are, therefore, asking every Negro to stay off the buses Monday in protest of the arrest and trial. Don't ride the buses to work, to town, to school, or anywhere on Monday. You can afford to stay out of school for one day if you have no other way to go except by bus. You can also afford to stay out of town for one day. If you work, take a cab, or walk. But please, children and grown-ups, don't ride the bus at all on Monday. Please stay off all buses Monday.[11]

Rather than the planned one day, the boycott lasted over a year until December 20, 1956, when the ruling in *Browder v. Gayle* ended Montgomery's segregated bus system. The next day, Montgomery's buses were integrated, but rather than joining in the celebration, Parks stayed home to tend to her ailing mother.[12] By then, much of the limelight was passing from Parks to Martin Luther King, Jr., but for many, Parks would always be the "Mother of the Modern Civil Rights Movement."

In his autobiography, King lists the Montgomery bus boycott as among those "outgrowths of [Henry David] Thoreau's insistence that evil must be resisted and that no moral man can patiently adjust to injustice." King argued that "noncooperation with evil is as much a moral obligation as is cooperation with good." Thoreau's concept of civil disobedience required an individual to "do at any time what I think right," regardless of what the majority may have deemed expedient. The white majority in Alabama had deemed segregation expedient, but Thoreau espoused that a man need not "resign his conscience to the legislation." Rosa Parks demonstrated that in such cases where a conflict exists, principles must decide.

Dorothea Dix and the Mentally Ill

Principle: "As ye would that men should do to you, do you even so to them."[13]

Lesson: Like all leadership, principled leadership is a process.

In May 1845, Dorothea Dix arrived in Illinois to continue the work she had already performed in several states on behalf of the mentally ill. After an extensive tour of the state, on January 11, 1847, she presented to the Illinois legislature a "memorial" that stressed the ethical obligation of society to care for its mentally ill. In making her appeal, Dix entreated the legislators to recall that "the Saviour, whose disciples we profess to be, left one simple, infallible rule, as a direction for the acts of man to his fellow-man, viz: '*as ye would that men should do to you, do you even so to them.*'"[14] For the student of principled leadership, Dix's statement is a wonderful example of how one woman cites a principle as not just a rule but as a call to action and a process.

In 1835, when she was 33 years old, Dix suffered a complete physical and psychological breakdown. She sought relief in a trip to Europe and spent much of 1836 and 1837 in Liverpool, England, with the family of William Rathbone, a socially conscious politician and reformer. It was through Rathbone that Dix came in contact with English modern ideas of prison and mental health reform and met with Samuel Tuke, founder of the York Retreat for the mentally ill.

Dix regained her health and returned to America just after the death of her grandmother. The inheritance Dix received allowed her to support herself independently and devote her time to charitable work. While teaching Sunday school classes to female convicts in East Cambridge Jail in 1841, Dix learned that not just criminals but also people with mental illnesses were housed in the jail because there was no other facility for them. She witnessed the terrible treatment these people received and resolved to improve their situation. Dix embarked on investigation of the treatment of the mentally ill in Massachusetts and in 1843 submitted her first "memorial" to the state legislature.[15] Dix's efforts enjoyed modest success in Massachusetts, and she expanded her work into New Jersey and Pennsylvania. In 1846, she turned her attention to Illinois, arriving there after a whirlwind tour of several southern states.

How the mentally ill were cared for in America in the 19th century was largely dependent on class. Those who had the financial means were often placed in private "asylums," which practiced a set of principles known as the "moral treatment" based on the work of Tuke in England, Benjamin Rush in the United States, and others. The moral treatment removed mentally ill persons from their present stressful environment and placed them in a benign but highly structured system of organized living under the close supervision of the superintendent, who was a physician. Patients followed regular schedules and routines and were kept occupied with activities such as crafts and gardening. Restraint was used as seldom as possible, but physicians did prescribe some sedatives, tonic, and, later, hydrotherapy. Many of these private asylums were at least loosely affiliated with church groups and included chapel services and other religious activities.[16]

The moral treatment seemed to work in the private asylums, but this level of care was not available to everyone. Those who were without such means were assigned to almshouses or poorhouses and jails, institutions neither designed for or able to treat mental illness but able to keep the unfortunate individuals "out of sight and out of mind" of the rest of society. A few reformers called for the states to take responsibility for the care of the mentally ill, but their efforts gained little traction with the general public and legislatures who were usually uninformed of the problems or of any possible solutions.[17] Dix's fact-finding expeditions and memorials were critical in raising consciousness of the terrible situation.

The process of principled leadership outlined in the Introduction begins with gathering the facts relevant to the situation, and this too is where Dix began her process.[18] While traveling to Illinois on a steamboat on the Mississippi River, Dix had met John King, a businessman from Jacksonville, Illinois. King told her of a campaign already under way to establish a hospital for the mentally ill in Jacksonville. Dix promised to visit Jacksonville soon but first proceeded to Alton where she visited the Illinois State Penitentiary. From there, she traveled to Galena, Rock Island, Nauvoo, Warsaw, Quincy, Columbus, Mount Sterling, and Meredosia in Illinois, along with brief sojourns to Kentucky and Iowa, before finally reaching Jacksonville.[19]

In Jacksonville, Dix contacted King, and his account of Dix's subsequent actions illustrates her energy and method. King reports that he met Dix at her hotel, and she immediately requested to visit the local jail and poorhouse. There, they "found a very violent, insane man by the name of Fanning, who was confined in a shallow cellar, 12 feet square, with a trap door, under the smoke house, and who was without clothing and straw for his bed, and was in a very filthy condition."

King persuaded Dix to stay at his home during her visit in Jacksonville, and Dix requested he invite "the leading citizens of the town to meet her in our parlor" so she could tell them of her mission. She then visited seven other counties in a one-horse buggy with King's brother Reynolds, "making her inquiries of citizens, on their way, for cases of insanity."[20] Dix found at least 300 insane persons in the jails and almshouses of central Illinois before heading north to places like Galena and then to several places in the southeastern part of the state. In June 1846, she was in Springfield before leaving Illinois for Missouri, Indiana, and Ohio. She became seriously ill in Columbus, and while she was convalescing, she organized her material before returning to Illinois. On January 11, 1847, she submitted a memorial to the 15th General Assembly of the state of Illinois that documented the history of mental hospitals and detailed her observations from her travels throughout Illinois.[21]

In the memorial, Dix uses language consistent with an appeal to principle. She tells the legislators, "I do not come to move your *benevolent* feelings, so much as to present just claims. I do not ask of you the performance of *generous* acts from yourselves and constituents, but respectfully urge you to fulfil *absolute obligations*: the obligations of man, favored with competence and sound reason, to his fellow-man, rendered helpless and dependent through infirmities to which *all* are exposed, and from which none are too rich to be exempt, or too poor to escape."[22] Attention has previously been called to William Safire's assertion that the basis of the word "principle" "came to mean a primary truth that formed the basis for other beliefs and then to mean a rule for ethical conduct." He points to principles as being "fixed, invariable, absolute, eternal."[23] Stephen Covey declares them to be "impersonal, factual, objective, and self-evident." He equates them to natural laws that operate constantly.[24] Consistent with these understandings, Dix describes her call to action not in terms of a request to be graciously granted as some voluntary option but as the just claim to the mandatory fulfillment of an existing obligation. So it is with principles. Once principled leaders ascertain the principles, they view the adherence to them not as extraordinary and negotiable exertions but as settled matters of fact. Principled leaders do not congratulate themselves for adhering to principles. They do not even consider not following them.[25]

For Dix, the principle at stake was "*as ye would that men should do to you, do you even so to them*," and after she had recounted the sufferings of so many mentally ill people, she asked the legislators to "place yourself for a few dreadful moments" in their situations. The "one effective remedy for these woes," she argued, was "a well established, skillfully conducted hospital."[26]

Principled leaders base their leadership actions on principles, without being distracted by other factors. However, the discussion of the process of principled leadership in the Introduction notes that if the action involves some ambiguity, friction, or compromise, the principled leader must determine how to mitigate that risk. Although not part of the principled leadership decision-making process, such consequences are real and must be reckoned with.[27]

In Dix's case, while opening a state-funded hospital was the solution her principle demanded, she also understood that for the legislators, budgetary constraints could not be ignored. To assuage these concerns, Dix chronicled how the moral treatment had proved more cost effective than providing lifelong custodial care in Ohio,

Massachusetts, and South Carolina, concluding that "humanity and economy are both largely concerned in the prompt and judicious treatment of the insane in the first stages of the disease."[28] Yet, for Dix, it was the principle at stake on which the legislators must base their decision. In the closing paragraph of her memorial, she challenges them to "rise not from the grave and often perplexing deliberations which claim your legislation, till you have added to acts bearing merely on the political condition of your State, this work of peremptory obligation to humanity."[29]

Dix's efforts achieved results. In his inaugural address on December 9, 1846, Governor Augustus French urged the Illinois legislature to make some provision for the mentally ill. Various proposals were then debated in the house and senate until agreement was reached on February 27, 1847, and a bill was passed to establish an Illinois State Hospital for the Insane in Jacksonville.[30]

Construction of the imposing facility began in the fall of 1847, and patients were admitted as various wings were completed. In the summer of 1852, the east wing was finished, the center section nearly so, and 80 patients were in residence. By the end of 1854, that number rose to 166. Authorizations for additional construction allowed the population to swell to 302 in 1862 and 406 in 1868. By the mid–1890s, the hospital consisted of two huge buildings and several smaller ones and housed over 1,200 patients.[31]

The phenomenal growth of the Jacksonville hospital came with its share of problems, including the difficulty in administering the close supervision and individual attention envisioned by the moral treatment to such a huge population.[32] Nonetheless, David Lightner provides a very powerful assessment of the difference Dix made, noting that for whatever its deficiencies, "in Dix's day, the state mental hospital was often a better refuge for the indigent insane than were the available alternatives—better than the road in Cass County along which a deranged old woman trudged on feet crippled by frostbite, better than the stifling jail cell at Springfield where a frenzied madman wallowed in his own filth, better than the barred cage within the Galena poorhouse where the cries of the insane denied rest to the poor and sick, and better by far than the pitch-dark pit where Fanning spent each lonely winter." This, Lightner writes, was "the cardinal legacy of the philanthropic lady and her errand of mercy to Illinois."[33]

In achieving this end, Dix provides an excellent example of how the process of principled leadership works. Through "arduous travel" conducted at an "exhausting pace," Dix gathered the facts.[34] As a Christian, she reviewed the principles found in the Bible and decided that "as ye would that men should do to you, do you even so to them" (Matthew 7:12) was the applicable one.[35] She articulated adherence to this principle as an "absolute obligation" that precluded any other possible responses.[36] She determined that the action associated with this principle was the building of a state hospital, and she presented her case to the legislature.[37] Although it did not impact on adherence to the principle, Dix recognized the costs associated with building a state hospital, and she addressed these concerns by explaining to the legislature the cost effectiveness of the moral treatment.[38] Through the use of the process of principled leadership, Dix defined a problem and saw through the implementation of its solution.

Denis Estimon and We Dine Together

Principle: Everyone should feel safe and accepted for who they are.

Lesson: Principled leaders create change to bring negative organizational values into alignment with positive ones.

Denis Estimon immigrated to the United States from Port-au-Prince, Haiti, when he was in the first grade. It was a difficult transition. Estimon recalls, "There was a language barrier ... and my mom was always working and my father was still in Haiti at the time so I wasn't able to talk to anybody. I felt isolated. I felt lonely." As a senior at Boca Raton Community High School in Florida, Estimon could "still remember how I felt not being able to speak to fellow students."[39] Along with Kinsley Soorestal, Allie Sealy, and Jean Max Meradie, Destimon decided to do something about it. They formed the We Dine Together movement to make sure that at lunchtime, everyone had a place they felt they belonged.

Estimon found his inspiration for We Dine Together in 2017 from his connection to Gregg Francis, director of People Reaching Out to Provide Education and Leadership (PROPEL), a nonprofit educational organization that serves economically depressed areas in and around Palm Beach County, Florida. PROPEL operates an educational center called the Hub where students can go after school. One day, Francis asked, "Does anybody on your campus, which is socioeconomically diverse, eat alone?" As Estimon pictured the cafeteria in his mind, he saw the popular, confident, and secure kids on one side and the "more isolated kids" on the other. He told Francis he didn't think it should be that way, and Francis told him, "You have an opportunity here to be leaders on your campus." As Estimon recalled, "He challenged me to do something about it and that's basically what I did."[40]

Most of Boca Raton's 3,400 students are white and come from financially stable families, but there are also minority students from some 70 countries, according to principal Susie King. The different ethnic or racial groups seldom mingle, so those from the smaller groups often find themselves isolated. Estimon notes that the sheer size of the student population can exacerbate the sense of being overwhelmed and alone.[41]

With the help of his English teacher, Jordan Hernandez, Estimon got the We Dine Together program started with an inaugural group of 15 students. By February, the club had over 100 members.[42] Hernandez describes the mission as being "to build relationships over the table. We try to go out and find those who are ostracized or isolated and bring them into the club." The goal is to create "a place where you are safe and accepted for who you are and for what you choose to be." According to Estimon, the feedback from the students was "tremendous."[43]

The club meets one lunch period a week in Hernandez's classroom for pizza and, as Hernandez describes it, to "do life with one another." It is a diverse group of "Latinos, black, white, some students that are Irish, Haitian students—all over the map," but Hernandez says, "they have one common goal and it's to make friends and understand each other."[44] The rest of the week, club members circulate throughout the school's courtyard joining and befriending students whom they find eating lunch alone.

Like Estimon, club cofounder Soorestal is from Haiti and remembers as a newcomer "what it's like to feel shy and by myself." "When my family moved here nine years ago, I was always the kid lunching alone. Now that I'm making a difference, it feels good to say, 'Hey, I gotcha, man. What's your name? How are you doing?'" "You can tell they really appreciate it," he says. "Maybe for the first time, they feel like they belong." Cofounder Sealy's family moved from Broward County her freshman year so she could go to Boca Raton High School. Although her move was a shorter one, she still recalls that "coming here, not knowing anyone, took a toll on my confidence. I became socially awkward. I sat by myself." Cofounder Meradieu eventually found his way onto the football team, but before that, he remembers, "Everybody else was laughing and having a good time, and I stood there, just watching. It was depressing." He "didn't want to go to school because I was so isolated from everybody." As a result of We Dine Together, Meradieu said he met kids he would never "ever" have met on the football team. The experience has been so powerful for him that he quit the football team so that he could spend more time with this club. He says, "I don't mind not getting a football scholarship. This is what I really want to do."[45]

One of Estimon's high school mentors was Ashleigh Cromer. Cromer is executive director of Be Strong, a nonprofit organization with the mission "to save and improve the lives of our youth using a peer-to-peer approach by strengthening mental, emotional, and relational health, building resilience, and preventing bullying." As We Dine Together grew, Estimon realized the program needed structure and organizational support. In 2018, We Dine Together became part of Be Strong, with Estimon assuming the position of "growth builder."[46]

Critical to this discussion of growth across all levels is an understanding of the connection between leadership and change. Peter Northouse notes that "the overriding function of management is to provide order and consistency to organizations, whereas the primary function of leadership is to produce change and movement. Management is about seeking order and stability, leadership is about seeking adaptive and constructive change."[47] Both leaders and managers need to understand *how things work*, but it is the leader who is driven *to make things work better*.[48] That is what Estimon set out to do.

The process of determining an organization's principles and infusing them in the organization, its leaders, and its members begins with developing an understanding of the organization's values. This step reveals what is important to the organization.[49] As Estimon surveyed his school, he determined that the organization valued social stratification and exclusivity. These organizational values were in conflict with his personal values of community and belongingness. Estimon drew on his principle that everyone should feel safe and accepted for who they are and, through the We Dine Together club, helped bring the school into alignment with that principle.

James Kouzes and Barry Posner note that "change is the work of leaders."[50] Northouse adds that leaders "act to expand the available options to long-standing problems" and "change the way people think about what is possible."[51] That is exactly what Estimon did. He looked around him and saw an unsatisfactory situation of isolation and loneliness. Then he pictured an alternative. "Imagine what would happen," he said, "if you had lunch with somebody new every day." The result would be "people com[ing] out of their shells and mak[ing] new friendships."[52] Reflecting on We Dine Together's success, Gregg Francis notes that "Denis and his friends decided to become true agents of change."[53] Creating change is what made Estimon a leader. That the change he created aligned the organization with a principle is what made him a principled leader.

Mohammad Gulab and Lokhay

Principle: Take the responsibility of safeguarding an individual against his or her enemies and protect him and her at all costs.

Lesson: A long-term shared cultural commitment can rally a community around its principles even under the most difficult circumstances.

On June 27, 2005, a four-man Navy SEAL team was inserted on the slopes of the Sawtalo Mountain in Kunar Province, Afghanistan, to gather intelligence about Ahmad Shah, leader of the Mountain Tigers, a guerrilla group aligned with the Taliban and other militant groups close to the Pakistani border. After the SEALs were compromised by coming in contact with some local goatherders,[54] a fierce firefight ensued in which three of the four members were killed. The surviving member, Hospital Corpsman Second Class (SEAL) Marcus Luttrell, was severely wounded but managed to travel seven miles on foot, evading the enemy for nearly a day.[55] Pashtun tribesmen of the village of Sabray, most notably Mohammad Gulab, came to Luttrell's aid and, in obedience to the principles of the ancient Pushtunwali code, cared for him and protected him from the Taliban until July 2 when he was rescued by U.S. forces.

After Luttrell's team members, Lieutenant Michael Murphy, Gunner's Mate Second Class (SEAL) Danny Dietz, and Sonar Technician Second Class (SEAL) Matthew Axelson were killed, Luttrell found himself badly wounded and alone. After a harrowing escape from the Taliban, he encountered a few Pashtuni tribesmen, led by a man named Sarawa, who turned out to be the village doctor. Sarawa gave Luttrell water and checked over his wound and then went into conference with his fellow villagers. As Luttrell describes it, "the decision Sarawa and his friends were making carried huge responsibilities and, possibly, momentous consequences: They had to decide whether to take me in. Whether to help me, shelter me, and feed me. Most importantly, whether to defend me."[56]

The Pashtuns are a fiercely independent people who live in the steep mountains of Afghanistan, completely outside of central government control. They have their own laws and they have their own ways, including the Pashtunwali code.[57] It was the principles of this code that would guide the people of Sabray in their dealings with Luttrell.

The Pashtunwali code is an unwritten code handed down from pre–Islamic times but all in concert with the teachings of Muhammad. There are 10 main principles. The two most applicable in Luttrell's situation were *melmastia* (hospitality) and *nanawatch* (asylum). *Melmastia* requires that hospitality and deep respect are extended to all visitors regardless of race, religion, national affiliation, or economic status. Moreover, this hospitality must be provided without any expectation of renumeration or favor. *Nanawatch* refers to protection given to a person against his enemies. People, including visitors, must be protected at all costs. Even those avoiding legal authorities must be given refuge until the situation can be clarified.[58]

Part of the Pashtunwali commitment to hospitality is captured in the idea of *lokhay warkawal*, which literally translated means "giving of a pot." Luttrell explains that for Sarawa and the rest of the village, the concept of *lokhay*

> carried many onerous responsibilities. *Lokhay* means not only providing care and shelter, it means an unbreakable commitment to defend that wounded man to the death. And not just the death of the principal tribesman or family who made the original commitment for the giving of a pot. It means the whole damned village. *Lokhay* means the population of that village will fight to the last man, honor-bound to protect the individual they have invited in to share their hospitality.... It's not a point of renegotiation. This is strictly nonnegotiable.[59]

Sarawa decided to follow the code. He cleaned Luttrell's wounds, removed shrapnel from his leg, and applied antiseptic cream and bandages. Then villagers gave Luttrell clean clothes and food and let him rest, but by now the Taliban knew Luttrell was in Sabray. Soon, eight armed Taliban fighters burst into Luttrell's room. One slapped him in the face, and they demanded information about American military operations and beat him. After about five hours of withstanding the Taliban threats, Luttrell reports that "a man who commanded colossal respect" entered the room. He was the village elder. He walked over to where Luttrell was lying, knelt down, gave him water and bread, and then turned to address the Taliban. Luttrell learned later that the man forbade the Taliban from taking Luttrell away. The man then exited the room, and the Taliban "suddenly decided to leave" as well.[60]

Sarawa arrived next and, with three armed guards, transported Luttrell out of the village to a cave. A guard named Norzamund was posted at the entrance. It was all a whirlwind experience, but Luttrell was beginning to sense that "Sarawa and his men were intent on saving me." "That," Luttrell explains, "is strictly *lokhay*."[61]

Before dawn on July 1, Norzamund and two other men got Luttrell from the cave and took him back to the village. There, Sarawa again treated Luttrell's wounds, and Luttrell was then moved to a house near the top of the village. "Soon after I arrived," writes Luttrell, "I met my first real friend, Mohammad Gulab, the thirty-three-year-old son of the village elder, and the resident police chief." According to Luttrell, Gulab "made it clear the Taliban were not going to take me while he had anything to do with it."[62]

Gulab's assurances came as it was becoming readily apparently to Luttrell that "I was a major problem to the village." Taliban fighters were threatening the villagers and demanding that Luttrell be surrendered to them immediately. This situation was explained to Luttrell by the village elder, Gulab's father, who also told him that a member of the tribe would travel to the U.S. base at Asadabad and inform the Americans there of Luttrell's whereabouts. Luttrell gave the elder a note to give the messenger, saying, "This man gave me shelter and food, and must be helped at all costs." Luttrell had no idea that it was the village elder himself who would deliver the message.[63]

While his father was making the trek, Gulab remained with Luttrell. The two communicated the best they could and got to know each other as human beings. Gulab had a village friend with him, and between the two of them, they never left Luttrell alone. By this time, Luttrell had learned that "the village was entirely embarrassed" by the earlier Taliban incursion and its affront to *lokhay*.[64]

On the morning of July 2, Luttrell was in great pain, and Gulab called for an old man who brought some tobacco opium that gave Luttrell much relief. He could also hear U.S. helicopters flying overhead. By now, Gulab had told Luttrell that it was his father who was walking to Asadabad alone. "All my hopes," recalled Luttrell, "rested in the soft tread of this powerful yet tiny old man."[65]

In the meantime, Luttrell recalls that Gulab "had now become the principal figure in my life," keeping Luttrell secure and fed.[66] While Gulab's father made his way to Asadabad, the Taliban stepped up their pressure on Sabray, demanding Luttrell be handed over to them immediately. When the Taliban finally did come, Gulab and the villagers rallied to Luttrell's defense. Luttrell describes Gulab's motivation as stemming from "a sense of honor that reached back down to generations, two thousand years of Pashtunwali tradition: You will defend your guest to the death."[67] Sabray's brave stance succeeded. The Taliban contented themselves with firing volleys of random shots into the air designed to frighten the villagers. They kept their distance and never attacked.[68]

Later, Luttrell and Gulab moved away from the village looking for a place where U.S. rescue helicopters might land. While on this mission, they encountered Ahmad Shah,[69] the very person Luttrell's SEAL team had been sent after, and his men. A tense standoff ensued, and Shah and Gulab stepped away to confer. When Gulab returned, he told Luttrell that Shah had handed him a note saying, "Either you hand over the American—or every member of your family will be killed."[70] By this point, Shah had returned to his men. He was giving Gulab one last chance because moments later, an Afghan special forces soldier followed by U.S. Army Rangers arrived on the scene. Luttrell's rescuers had arrived.[71]

Both Gulab and Luttrell were evacuated by helicopter to Asadabad. Gulab remained there, and Luttrell transferred to a C-130 that took him to Bagram.[72] Luttrell's long ordeal was over, and he had Gulab and the village of Sabray to thank for it. During those seven days, Luttrell recalls, "I could have died about nine more deaths. Gulab saved me, and on every occasion, he put his own life on the line, facing down inevitable death himself."[73]

X. Jasmine Bordere and Franklin Mixon assert that the Pashtunwali code created a community "ethos" of "principles [that] are nurtured from 'childhood to death.'"[74] As did James Burke's credo at Johnson & Johnson, the Pashtunwali code created a culture in the village of Sabray. *Lokhay* tied the fate of the entire village to Luttrell, whatever the risks. That these principles were infused in the Pashtun people throughout centuries of adherence to the code allowed them to follow it, individually and collectively, even under life-threatening circumstances.

Conclusion

The first purpose of this book is to lend some rigor and distinguishability to principled leadership as a leadership theory. The Introduction reviewed the literature and attempted to answer the question, "What is principled leadership?" The second goal is to champion the value of principled leadership by providing positive examples of its use. The book attempted to do this through case studies drawn from business, political, military, religious, sports, literary, and societal leaders. From these case studies, certain commonalities have emerged that may provide some insights into a set of principles around which principled leaders might rally. As a starting point, let's return to Hendrikz and Engelbrecht's list of "universal moral values."

1. Commitment to something greater than oneself.
2. Trustworthiness.
3. Respect for self, human race, the environment, and other living beings.
4. Responsibility.
5. Fairness.
6. Caring.
7. Citizenship.[1]

Many of the case studies represent more than one of these seven values, but some of the strongest linkages follow.

Several case studies demonstrated "commitment to something greater than oneself." Father Damien was willing to contract leprosy himself in order to serve others. Herb Kelleher's philosophy was to put his employees first, even if that meant losing money by not having furloughs. John Boyd put making a difference ahead of his own career progression. John McCain refused early release as a POW because the Code of Conduct required it of him. Mahatma Gandhi pursued satyagraha even though it meant self-suffering. Eric Liddell forfeited his chance of winning a gold medal by not competing on Sunday. Daniel, Shadrach, Meshach, and Abednego obeyed God rather than secular rulers, even at the risk of their lives.

"Trustworthiness" was represented by Katumba Wamala, Atticus Finch, and Bobby Jones. By consistently subordinating politics to peace, Wamala won the trust of an anxious citizenry. By his faithful representation of Tom Robinson, Finch won the trust of the Black community in Maycomb. By enforcing rules on himself, even when no one was watching, Bobby Jones earned the trust of his competitors.

John Hall, James Burke, and Charles Spaulding modelled crisis and social "responsibility" in corporate settings. Those men were in a position that gave them an opportunity to fulfill their duties in a responsible manner. Other case studies involved individuals who were not in such a position but who saw a need and then assumed responsibility. These include Rosa Parks who assumed the role of "Mother of the Modern Civil Rights Movement," George Marshall who said yes to each successive responsibility the president asked of him, and Jim who took responsibility for Huck when Huck needed a father figure. In fact, it does not take too much imagination to describe every one of the case studies as reflecting someone taking responsibility for something.

Because "citizenship" involves the fulfillment of the responsibilities of being a citizen, there are several intersections between the values of citizenship and responsibility. George Marshall, for example, modeled good citizenship in fulfilling the responsibilities to which the president appointed him. Juror Number 8 modeled good citizenship in fulfilling his civic duty as a juror. Jiggs Casey modeled good citizenship by supporting the U.S. Constitution's subordination of the military to civilian authority.

Examples of "respect for self, human race, the environment and other living beings" take many forms. Respect for self is present in Herb Kelleher's philosophy to "be yourself." Respect for the human race and other living beings often manifested itself in protecting others. Carl Lutz protected the Hungarian Jews. Rachael Denhollander protected victims of sexual abuse. Hugh Thompson protected noncombatants. Mohammad Gulab protected a stranger. Respect for the environment was represented by John Hall's response to the Ashland Oil spill.

In many ways, "fairness" was indirectly represented in each case involving respect for other living beings, but there were several cases in which that respect was very directly tied to fairness. Rosa Parks and Abraham Lincoln demanded fair treatment for Black people. Thich Quang Do wanted Buddhists to be treated fairly. James created conditions for Gentiles to be treated fairly. Bobby Jones treated his opponents fairly. Juror Number 8 treated the accused fairly. Mahatma Gandhi sought fair treatment for Indians.

"Caring" also manifested itself as respect in action. Denis Estimon cared for his isolated schoolmates. Atticus Finch cared for Tom Robinson. Jim cared for Huck. Dorothea Dix cared for the mentally ill. Father Damien cared for the lepers. Armando Galarraga cared for Jim Joyce. Like responsibility, every case study can easily be described as someone caring for something or somebody.

The result, then, is that Hendrikz and Engelbrecht's list of "universal moral values" can be used to categorize these case studies. But as noted in the Introduction, values and principles are not the same thing, and declaring something "universal" based on 28 case studies is problematic. Nonetheless, in an effort to advance the discussion and, hopefully, the scholarship, this study suggests its own list of universal principles, informed by the values put forth by Hendrikz and Engelbrecht. Based on wisdom presented earlier by Stanley Porter suggesting to impose the minimum, not the maximum[2] and by Anna Simons to keep principled leadership empowering rather than proscriptive,[3] as well as the inherent difficulty in determining "universal" principles, only three are offered.

The first is based on Hendrikz and Engelbrecht's "commitment to something greater than oneself" but endeavors to remove the subjectivity from that particular wording. Committing to something greater than oneself simply allows too much subjectivity both in the assessment and the choice. There are many things that are greater than each of us and committing to one of those does not create the absolute nature of a principle. What if there is something greater still than the thing to which we have decided to commit? Could that not present a potential conflict if we had to make a decision involving a choice between those greater and lesser things? Should we not instead commit to what is the "greatest" thing rather than simply something "greater"? If that logic is accepted, the problem still remains of determining what is universally accepted as the greatest thing. Setting aside that discussion for another time and place, "commit to the highest moral and legitimate authority" captures the essence and is offered as Principle #1.

Principle #2 aims to capture Hendrikz and Engelbrecht's emphasis on trustworthiness, respect, caring, and fairness. All these values relate to how we treat other people and reflect what we generally consider to be the Golden Rule of treating other people as we would like to be treated ourselves. Marshall Goldsmith, however, has made the compelling argument that a better standard might be to treat others as *they* would like to be treated. His logic is that we all have different levels of tolerance for life's inconsistencies, annoyances, and difficulties. If it is within our ability to absorb some circumstance, we sometimes have a hard time understanding why other people can't also just suck it up and deal with it. Real understanding of others requires us to see things not from our point of view but from the other person's, and leaders must remember that they are leading other people, not themselves.[4] With Goldsmith's wisdom in mind, Principle #2 is "Treat other people as they would like to be treated."

Principle #3 addresses responsibility and citizenship from Hendrikz and Engelbrecht's list. Whether to ourselves, our family, our job, our boss, our community, our nation, or our world, responsibility and citizenship require us to do our duty. Freshmen at The Citadel are required to memorize a quotation attributed to Robert E. Lee: "Duty is the *sublimest word* in the language. You should do your duty in all things. You can never do more. You should never wish to do less."[5] It is with that comprehensive approach to duty in mind that Principle #3 is "Do your legal and moral duty in all things."

1. Commit to the highest moral and legitimate authority.
2. Treat other people as they would like to be treated.
3. Do your legal and moral duty in all things.

These three principles are offered as a common point of departure for any principled leader to apply to his or her situation and then add (or not) additional specifics as necessary. I would suggest, however, that principled leadership is at its best when "less is more." The effort to determine principles cannot give way to legalism. In reality, if the leader can build in his or her followers the commitment to the highest moral and legitimate authority, it would seem that everything else would pretty much take care of itself. St. Augustine seemed to subscribe to this philosophy when he preached, "Love God and do whatever you please."[6]

Appendix 1

CADRE Beliefs, Values, and Principles[1]

Beliefs

CADRE was founded with a set of beliefs that has guided us to this day, and has formed the basis of everything we do. We BELIEVE that:

- Every parent or caregiver in South LA is a valuable asset of the community.
- Each parent or caregiver in South LA is capable of being a leader for social change.
- Raising a child in South LA is a political act: helping children discover their self-worth and life options in an environment of racist oppression and repression takes incredible resistance to negative forces and constant negotiation with power for the most basic of needs.
- The quality of life in South LA depends almost entirely on the quality of its schools. As a public we will only achieve real education reform when parents have real power.
- The community will develop if the schools develop collective consciousness and solidarity among their students and parents. This requires resistance to labeling, tracking, dividing, and intensifying competition between children and parents along racial, economic, language, behavioral, or ability lines in order to separate children and families into economic winners and losers.

- Regardless of income, South LA parents are the true owners of public education: without them there would be no schools.
- Every person has the human rights to a quality education, dignity, and participation in the institutions that affect them.

Values

Because of these beliefs, we most value:

- Parent leadership development and power
- Cultivation and collection of parent knowledge
- Parent decision-making
- Dignity and respect for parents
- Organizational democracy
- Collective struggle and identity
- Liberation from racism
- Social justice rooted in human rights: civil, political, economic, social, and cultural
- Accountability and responsibility
- Preservation of public education

Principles

So that our work consistently reflects our beliefs and values, we operate with the following principles:

- Primary members are parents/caregivers whose children attend public schools in the South LA region of the Los Angeles Unified School District.
- We strive for a membership equally balanced among African American and Latino parents, regardless of the demographics of schools and out of deep respect for both the shared and distinct histories and experiences in South LA.
- We remove language, transportation, and childcare barriers to every extent possible.
- Our members have the access, tools, support, and time they need to make the most informed, well thought-out decisions to direct the organization's strategies and goals.

CADRE Beliefs, Values, and Principles

- We create and fulfill opportunities for all of our members to engage in a deep understanding of power and spheres of influence within the public systems that control the quality of their lives.
- Our work challenges the status quo of parent-school relationships at every opportunity and remains vigilant about our mission and vision.
- Our organization maintains independence and autonomy in order to maximize the power of our members to speak their truths and demand true community-driven solutions and public accountability.
- We learn from social change movement victories and shortcomings, past and present, in order to find the most promising strategies and tactics for building long-term power.
- We regularly evaluate the quality of our relationships and decisions, and our accountability to our members.

Appendix 2

Master List of Principles and Lessons

James Burke and the Tylenol Recall

Principle: "Put the needs and well-being of the people we serve first."

Lesson: Once an organizational culture of principled leadership is established, the system largely runs itself.

John Hall and the Ashland Oil Spill

Principle: Take responsibility for and fix your mistakes.

Lesson: When an organization finds itself out of alignment with its principles, restore alignment as directly as possible.

Charles Spaulding and Cardinal Point No. 4

Principle: "There must be social service in business."

Lesson: The discipline of thoughtfully and deliberately listing principles is fundamental to the practice of principled leadership.

Herb Kelleher and Leadership Philosophy

Principle: "Be yourself."

Lesson: A philosophy of leadership informs the way a leader will use his or her principles to influence others.

George Marshall and the Mission to China

Principle: If the president asks, do it.

Lesson: Principles help resolve moral dilemmas.

Carl Lutz and the Hungarian Jews

Principle: Protect the defenseless.

Lesson: Principled leaders influence others to emulate their behavior.

Abraham Lincoln and Emancipation

Principle: "The paramount object in [the U.S. Civil War] is to save the Union."

Lesson: Even principled leaders must be pragmatic.

Mahatma Gandhi and Satyagraha

Principle: "Pursuit of truth [does] not admit of violence being inflicted on one's opponent but that he must be weaned from error by patience and sympathy ... and patience means self-suffering."

Lesson: Precommit to follow your principles.

John McCain and Being a Prisoner of War

Principle: "I will accept neither parole nor special favors from the enemy."

Lesson: Organizations build alignment through training.

Katumba Wamala and Trust

Principle: "There is nothing as important as peace."

Lesson: The consistency of principled leadership helps build trust.

John Boyd and Careerism

Principle: You must choose to either be someone or do something.

Lesson: Principled leadership requires commitment to something bigger than yourself.

Hugh Thompson and My Lai

Principle: "These people were looking at me for help and there was no way I could turn my back on them."

Lesson: The influence of a principled leader can be both direct and immediate as well as indirect and delayed.

Daniel, Shadrach, Meshach, and Abednego and Fixed Principles

Principle: Serve and worship God alone.

Lesson: The fixed and objective nature of principles provides clarity and constancy amid change.

Thich Quang Do and Speaking Truth to Power

Principle: "Then and there I vowed to do all that I could to combat fanaticism and intolerance and devote my life to the pursuit of justice through the Buddhist teachings of nonviolence, tolerance and compassion."

Lesson: Speak truth to power in a virtuous way.

Father Damien and the Leper Colony at Kalaupapa

Principle: "I would like to sacrifice myself for the poor lepers."

Lesson: Servant leadership and principled leadership are not the same thing, but there are points of intersection.

James and the Jerusalem Council

Principle: "The remnant of men may seek the Lord, and all the Gentiles who bear my name, says the Lord, who does these things that have been known for ages."

Lesson: When it comes to compromise, context matters. Compromising in a relationship may be good, but compromising principles is not.

Eric Liddell and the 1924 Olympics

Principle: "I object to Sunday sport in toto."

Lesson: Although adherence to principles can come with some costs, it is also very liberating in the sense that it simplifies a leader's decision-making.

Bobby Jones and the 1925 U.S. Open

Principle: "There is only one way to play this game."

Lesson: Personal power, earned by the setting of example, is an effective means of influence for the principled leader.

Armando Galarraga and the 28-Out Perfect Game

Principle: "The umpire is in charge."

Lesson: "Nobody's perfect."

Rachael Denhollander and Helping Others Find Their Voice

Principle: "How much is a little girl worth? ... 'Everything' is what these survivors are worth."

Lesson: When leading by example, principled leaders model principles in a way that helps others find their voice about the principles.

Atticus Finch and Empathy

Principle: "You never really understand a person until you consider things from his point of view—until you climb into his skin and walk around in it."

Lesson: Principled leadership should be worthy of emulation.

Jim and Principled Leadership Based on Personal Authority

Principle: "We do not know much about Jim, but we do know that he has great love for his family and longs for the day when he will be free in order to reclaim them. In the meantime, Huck is his family."

Lesson: The practice of principled leadership is not dependent on positional authority.

Jiggs Casey and Civilian Control of the Military

Principle: Civilian control of the military

Lesson: Principles help people navigate divided loyalties.

Juror Number 8 and a Fair Trial

Principle: Innocent until proven guilty.

Lesson: Principled leaders "lift people out of their petty preoccupations and unite them toward higher ends."

Rosa Parks and the Montgomery Bus Boycott

Principle: "It was unfair to segregate us."

Lesson: Principles transcend values.

Dorothea Dix and the Mentally Ill

Principle: "As ye would that men should do to you, do you even so to them."

Lesson: Like all leadership, principled leadership is a process.

Denis Estimon and We Dine Together

Principle: Everyone should feel safe and accepted for who they are.

Lesson: Principled leaders create change to bring negative organizational values into alignment with positive ones.

Mohammad Gulab and Lokhay

Principle: Take the responsibility of safeguarding an individual against his or her enemies and protect him or her at all costs.

Lesson: A long-term shared cultural commitment can rally a community around its principles even under the most difficult circumstances.

Chapter Notes

Preface

1. *Cadet Leader Development Program*, 3rd ed. (Charleston, SC: The Citadel, 2017), 3.
2. John Grinalds, "Developing Leaders at the Citadel," *Command* 47, no. 1 (1998): 6.
3. *Catalog of the Citadel 2003–2004* (Charleston, SC: The Citadel, 2003), 10–11.
4. *A Guide for the Leader Development Program* (Charleston, SC: The Citadel, 2014), 2.
5. *Cadet Leader Development Program*, 5.
6. Peter Northouse, *Leadership: Theory and Practice*, 8th ed. (Thousand Oaks: Sage, 2019), 3.

Introduction

1. Peter Northouse, *Leadership: Theory and Practice*, 8th ed. (Thousand Oaks: Sage, 2019), 5.
2. *Merriam-Webster's Collegiate Dictionary*, 11th ed. (Springfield, MA: Merriam-Webster, 2020), 327.
3. Karen Hendrikz and Amos Engelbrecht, "The Principled Leadership Scale: An Integration of Value-Based Leadership," *SA Journal of Industrial Psychology* 45 (March 2019): 4.
4. Stephen Covey, *Principle-Centered Leadership* (New York: Fireside, 1992), 18.
5. *Ibid.*, 25.
6. Manuel London, "Principled Leadership and Business Diplomacy: A Practical, Values-Based Direction for Management Development," *Journal of Management Development* 18, no. 2 (1999): 172.
7. William Safire, "On Language: Principles vs Values," *New York Times*, August 12, 1984, section 6, 8.
8. The Citadel, *Leader Development Program* (Charleston, SC: The Citadel, 2014), 2.
9. Robert Daft, *The Leadership Experience*, 6th ed. (Stamford, CT: Cengage, 2015), 447.
10. Isaac Prilleltensky, "Value-Based Leadership in Organizations: Balancing Values, Interests, and Power among Citizens, Workers, and Leaders," *Ethics & Behavior* 10, no. 2 (2000): 139.
11. Michael Dantley, "Principled, Pragmatic, and Purposive Leadership: Reimagining Educational Leadership through Prophetic Spirituality," *Journal of School Leadership* 13, no. 2 (March 2003): 190.
12. Robert Birnbaum describes "loose coupling" as "connections between organizational subsystems that may be infrequent, circumscribed, weak in their mutual effects, unimportant, or slow to respond." See Robert Birnbaum, *How Colleges Work* (San Francisco: Jossey-Bass, 1988), 38.
13. London, "Principled Leadership and Business Diplomacy," 185.
14. Maryann Glynn and Heather Jamerson, "Principled Leadership: A

Framework for Action," in *Leading with Values: Positivity, Virtue and High Performance*, ed. E.D. Hess and K.S. Cameron (Cambridge: Cambridge University Press, 2006), 151.

15. *Ibid.*, 164–165.

16. *Ibid.*, 169.

17. James Kouzes and Barry Posner, *The Leadership Challenge: How to Make Extraordinary Things Happen in Organizations*, 5th ed. (New York: Wiley, 2012), 49.

18. Joseph Badaracco, *Questions of Character: Illuminating the Heart of Leadership through Literature* (Boston: Harvard Business Review Press, 2006), 140.

19. *Ibid.*

20. London, "Principled Leadership and Business Diplomacy," 172, 174.

21. Anna Simons, "Backbone vs. Box: The Choice between Principled and Prescriptive Leadership," in *The Future of the Army Profession*, ed. L. Matthews (New York: McGraw-Hill, 2002), 391.

22. *Ibid.*, 379–380.

23. Lynn Paine, "Managing for Organizational Integrity," *Harvard Business Review*, March 1, 1994, 107.

24. Gene Klann, *The Application of Power and Influence in Organizational Leadership* (Fort Leavenworth, KS: CGSC, 2010), 2.

25. *Ibid.*, 5.

26. *Ibid.*, 10.

27. Gary Yukl, *Leadership in Organizations* (Upper Saddle River: Pearson, 2010), 155.

28. Klann, 2.

29. Gary Yukl and Cecilia Falbe, "Influence Tactics in Upward, Downward, and Lateral Influence Attempts," *Journal of Applied Psychology* 75, no. 2 (1990): 132.

30. Klann, *Application of Power and Influence*, 5.

31. *Ibid.*, 6.

32. *Ibid.*, 7.

33. *Ibid.*, 1.

34. Yukl, *Leadership in Organizations*, 153.

35. Klann, *Application of Power and Influence*, 6–8.

36. Covey, *Principle-Centered Leadership*, 98.

37. London, "Principled Leadership and Business Diplomacy," 171, 179.

38. *Ibid.*, 179.

39. Gary Yukl, Cecilia Falbe, and Joo Young Yoon, "Patterns of Influence for Managers," *Group & Organization Management* 18, no. 1 (March 1993): 7.

40. Robert Cialdini, *Influence: Science and Practice* (Needham Heights, MA: Allyn & Bacon, 2009), vi–vii.

41. *Ibid.*, 143.

42. *Ibid.*, 164.

43. *Ibid.*, 44–45.

44. Covey, *Principle-Centered Leadership*, 119–129.

45. *Ibid.*, 119.

46. Northouse, *Leadership*, 5.

47. Covey, *Principle-Centered Leadership*, 122.

48. Ruth Bernheim and Alan Melnick, "Principled Leadership in Public Health: Integrating Ethics into Practice and Management," *Journal of Public Health Management & Practice* 14, no. 4 (July/August 2008): 362.

49. *Ibid.*, 364–365.

50. Northouse, *Leadership*, 4.

51. London, "Principled Leadership and Business Diplomacy," 186.

52. *Ibid.*

53. *Ibid.*, 175.

54. Michael Brown, Linda Treviño, and David Harrison, "Ethical Leadership: A Social Learning Perspective for Construct Development and Testing," *Organizational Behavior and Human Decision Processes* 97, no. 2 (July 2005): 120.

55. Bill George, *Discover Your True North* (New York: Wiley, 2015), 107.

56. Stephen Covey, *The 8th Habit: From Effectiveness to Greatness* (New York: Free Press, 2004), 49.

57. Safire, "On Language."

58. Covey, *8th Habit*, 49.

59. Safire, "On Language."

60. Covey, *8th Habit*, 46–49.

61. Quoted in Safire, "On Language."

62. Covey, *8th Habit*, 49.

63. Ken Shelton, "Principled

Leadership," *Leadership Excellence* 26 (May 2009): 6.

64. Hendrikz and Engelbrecht, "The Principled Leadership Scale," 2.

65. *Ibid.*, 2.

66. See "A Short List of Universal Morals."

67. See "Universal Moral Values for Corporate Codes of Ethics."

68. Louis Pojman and James Fieser, *Ethics: Discovering Right and Wrong* (Stamford, CT: Cengage, 2011), 39–40.

69. Scott Curry, Daniel Mullins, and Harvey Whitehouse, "Is It Good to Cooperate? Testing the Theory of Morality-as-Cooperation in 60 Societies," *Current Anthropology* 60, no. 1 (February 2019).

70. Kent Keith, *Morality and Morale: A Business Tale* (Honolulu: Terrace Press, 2012).

71. As argued previously, principles, not values, are the operative element of "principled" leadership, but as John Gardner explains, "if leaders cannot find in their constituencies any base of shared values, principled leadership becomes nearly impossible." John Gardner, *On Leadership* (New York: Free Press, 1990), 113.

72. George, *Discover Your True North*, 226; Kouzes and Posner, *The Leadership Challenge*, 46.

73. Glynn and Jamerson, "Principled Leadership," 165–166; John Rubino, "Aligning Personal Values and Corporate Values: A Personal and Strategic Necessity," *Employment Relations Today*, Autumn 1998, 33.

74. Paine, "Managing for Organizational Integrity," 115.

75. Kouzes and Posner, *The Leadership Challenge*, 57–69.

76. *Ibid.*, 87–95.

77. Gardner, *On Leadership*, 192.

78. Markkula Center for Applied Ethics at Santa Clara University, "A Framework for Ethical Decision Making," https://www.scu.edu/ethics/ethics-resources/ethical-decision-making/a-framework-for-ethical-decision-making/. Glynn and Jamerson write that "as an initial step, leaders must become aware of the moral and ethical dimensions of a particular situation, and evaluate the extent to which the existing conceptual models attend to these moral and ethical issues." Glynn and Jamerson, "Principled Leadership," 165.

79. Step 2 of Glynn and Jamerson's three-step process of principled leadership is "self-reflection on one's personal values, the firm's values, and their alignment." Glynn and Jamerson, "Principled Leadership," 164–165.

80. Step 1 of Glynn and Jamerson's three-step process of principled leadership is "awareness, making moral and ethical dimensions an explicit part of leadership decisions and action." Glynn and Jamerson, "Principled Leadership," 164–165.

81. James Kouzes and Barry Posner write that options contrary to the leader's core values "are seldom considered or acted on; and if they are, it's done with a sense of compliance rather than commitment." Kouzes and Posner, *The Leadership Challenge*, 49.

82. Kidder writes that moral courage, which is "driven by principles," "depends on an ability to elevate one or more key values above others." Rushworth Kidder, *Moral Courage* (New York: William Morrow, 2005), 10, 106.

83. Isaac Prilleltensky notes that one risk faced by value-based leaders is "to remain at a level of abstraction that makes for an internally coherent set of values but that is of little use in practice. Values have to be articulated in such a way that they can be translated into concrete policies and guidelines." Prilleltensky, "Value-Based Leadership," 151.

84. Anna Simons describes principled leadership as a very empowering form of leadership that makes available to the leader a host of options, so long as they are consistent with the values. Simons, "Backbone vs. Box," 379.

85. Paine, "Managing for Organizational Integrity," 115; Markkula Center, "Framework."

86. Markkula Center, "Framework." Kidder writes that we must "find the most

important principle to uphold—not necessarily because we think it will produce the best outcomes, but because it's the right thing to do regardless of the consequences." Kidder, *Moral Courage*, 145.

87. Badaracco argues that "combining principles and pragmatism is among the most difficult challenges leaders face." Badaracco, *Questions of Character*, 140.

88. Michael Dantley notes that "principled leadership is demonstrated through reflective, ethical decision making, which is a process where principled leaders interrogate their motivation as well as the projected results of their decisions." Dantley, "Principled, Pragmatic, and Purposive Leadership," 190.

89. Prilleltensky writes, "To enhance the level of accountability in the process of value clarification, I recommend that leaders consult with colleagues and others knowledgeable in the area of values." Prilleltensky, "Value-Based Leadership," 151.

90. Number 22 of Covey's "thirty means of influence" is "recognize and take time to teach."

91. Simons, "Backbone vs. Box," 379.

92. https://www.merriam-webster.com/dictionary/principle.

93. Gardner, *On Leadership*, 116.

94. *Cadet Leader Development Program*, 5.

95. *Ibid.*, 3.

96. *Ibid.*, 5.

97. Beliefs, Values & Principles—CADRE (cadre-la.org).

Case Studies

Business Leaders

1. Johnson & Johnson, "Our Credo," https://www.jnj.com/about-jnj/jnj-credo.

2. *Ibid.*

3. Unless otherwise noted, the following discussion of Burke's handling of the Tylenol poisoning crisis comes from "The Chairman: James Burke," Canal de IAETA, https://www.youtube.com/watch?v=N2MSmOqcQb4.

4. Rushworth Kidder, *How Good People Make Tough Choices* (New York: Harper, 1995), 80.

5. Craig Johnson, *Meeting the Ethical Challenges of Leadership* (Los Angeles: Sage, 2018), 348.

6. Kidder, *How Good People*, 81.

7. *Ibid.*

8. Lynn Paine, "Managing for Organizational Integrity," *Harvard Business Review*, March 1, 1994, 110.

9. *Ibid.*, 115.

10. *Ibid.*, 107.

11. Mukul Pandya, *Lasting Leadership* (Upper Saddle River: Prentice Hall, 2005), 39.

12. Kidder, *How Good People*, 81.

13. Pandya, *Lasting Leadership*, 43.

14. Craig Johnson, *Meeting the Ethical Challenges of Leadership* (Los Angeles: Sage, 2018), 415.

15. Lynn Perry Wooten and Erika Hayes James, "Linking Crisis Management and Leadership Competencies: The Role of Human Resource Development," *Advances in Developing Human Resources* 10, no. 3 (June 2008): 366.

16. Anne Delehunt, "Ashland Oil Inc.: Trouble at Floreffe (A)," *Harvard Business Review*, January 19, 1990, 5.

17. *Ibid.*, 3–4.

18. Markkula Center for Applied Ethics at Santa Clara University, "A Framework for Ethical Decision Making," https://www.scu.edu/ethics/ethics-resources/ethical-decision-making/a-framework-for-ethical-decision-making/.

19. Joyce West, "John Hall: The Kentucky Commodore," Kentucky Educational Television, April 27, 2016, https://www.pbs.org/video/ket-documentaries-john-hall-kentucky-commodore/.

20. Delehunt, "Ashland Oil Inc.," 6.

21. West, "John Hall."

22. Johnson, *Meeting the Ethical Challenges*, 431.

23. Daryl Koehen, "Why Saying 'I'm Sorry' Isn't Good Enough: The Ethics of Corporate Apologies," *Business Ethics Quarterly* 23, no. 2 (April 2013): 254.

24. Kevin Dougherty, *Leadership*

Lessons from the Vicksburg Campaign (Philadelphia: Casemate, 2011), 59.

25. Delehunt, "Ashland Oil Inc.," 8.

26. West, "John Hall."

27. *Ibid.*

28. Johnson, *Meeting the Ethical Challenges*, 425.

29. *Ibid.*

30. Anna Simons, "Backbone vs. Box: The Choice between Principled and Prescriptive Leadership," in *The Future of the Army Profession*, ed. L. Matthews (New York: McGraw-Hill 2002), 391.

31. "Ashland Accepts Oil Spill Accord," *New York Times*, September 9, 1989, https://www.nytimes.com/1989/11/09/us/ashland-accepts-oil-spill-accord.html.

32. West, "John Hall."

33. Leon Prieto and Simone Phipps, *African American Management History: Insights on Gaining a Cooperative Advantage* (Bingley, UK: Emerald, 2019), 101.

34. *Ibid.*, 63, 95, 101.

35. *Cambridge Business English Dictionary* (Cambridge: Cambridge University Press, 2011).

36. Prieto and Phipps, *African American Management History*, 102.

37. *Ibid.*, 64–66.

38. *Ibid.*, 65.

39. Walter Weare, "Spaulding, Charles Clinton," in *Dictionary of North Carolina Biography*, ed. William Powell (Chapel Hill: University of North Carolina Press, 1994), 408.

40. Prieto and Phipps, *African American Management History*, 66.

41. *Oxford Advanced Learner's Dictionary* (New York: Oxford University Press, 2020).

42. William Safire, "On Language: Principles vs Values," *New York Times*, August 12, 1984, section 6, 8. See Introduction: What Is Principled Leadership?

43. Prieto and Phipps, *African American Management History*, 67, 70.

44. *Ibid.*, 68.

45. Weare, "Spaulding, Charles Clinton," 408.

46. Prieto and Phipps, *African American Management History*, 77.

47. *Ibid.*, 77, 83.

48. *Ibid.*, 74.

49. *Ibid.*

50. *Ibid.*, 71.

51. *Ibid.*, 76, 102.

52. *Ibid.*, 83.

53. Weare, "Spaulding, Charles Clinton," 408.

54. Safire, "On Language," 8.

55. Herb Kelleher, "The Best Lesson in Leadership," in *Leader to Leader*, ed. Frances Hesselbein and Paul Cohen (San Francisco: Jossey-Bass, 1999), 43.

56. Quoted in Harry Garner, "Developing an Effective Command Philosophy," *Military Review*, September–October, 2012, 77.

57. *Ibid.*, 43.

58. *Ibid.*, 44.

59. Subruta Chakravarty, "Hit 'em Hardest with the Mostest," *Forbes*, September 16, 1991.

60. Kelleher, "The Best Lesson," 44.

61. Garner, "Developing an Effective Command Philosophy," 76.

62. Chakravarty, "Hit 'em Hardest."

63. *Ibid.*

64. Joe Nocera, "The Sinatra of Southwest Feels the Love," *New York Times*, May 24, 2008.

65. Kelleher, "The Best Lesson," 46.

66. *Ibid.*, 44.

67. Karen Hendrikz and Amos Engelbrecht, "The Principled Leadership Scale: An Integration of Value-Based Leadership," *SA Journal of Industrial Psychology* 45 (March 2019): 2.

68. James Hunter, *The Servant: A Simple Story about the True Essence of Leadership* (New York: Crown Currency, 1998), 125.

69. Kevin Frieberg and Jackie Freiberg, "20 Reasons Why Herb Kelleher Was One of the Most Beloved Leaders of Our Time," *Forbes*, January 4, 2019.

70. Stephen Breyer, "Airline Deregulation Revisited," *Business Week*, January 20, 2011.

71. Nocera, "The Sinatra of Southwest."

72. Rodd Wagner, "How Herb's Heart Still Beats at Southwest," *Forbes*, January 27, 2019, https://www.forbes.com/sites/roddwagner/2019/01/27/how-herbs-heart-still-beats-at-southwest/?sh=59110c9ecc8e.
73. Kelleher, "The Best Lesson," 44.
74. *Ibid.*, 46.
75. *Ibid.*, 47.
76. Chakravarty, "Hit 'em Hardest."
77. *Ibid.*
78. See discussions of Kouzes and Posner, Covey, Klann, and Yukl in the Introduction.
79. Kelleher, "The Best Lesson," 46.
80. *Ibid.*, 50.
81. Chakravarty, "Hit 'em Hardest."
82. Kelleher, "The Best Lesson," 44.
83. Hendrikz and Engelbrecht, 4. See the Introduction.
84. Garner, "Developing an Effective Command Philosophy," 77.
85. Chris Isidore, "Southwest Explains Its Meltdown to Congress," CNN.com, February 9, 2023.
86. Beth Kowitt, "Southwest's Biggest Mistake Was Forgetting Its Own Culture," *Washington Post*, December 31, 2022.
87. *Ibid.*
88. James Collins, *Good to Great* (New York: Harper Business, 2001), 130.

Political Leaders

1. Maryann Glynn and Heather Jamerson, "Principled Leadership: A Framework for Action," in *Leading with Values: Positivity, Virtue and High Performance*, E.D. Hess and K.S. Cameron (Cambridge: Cambridge University Press, 2006), 151.
2. Forrest Pogue, *George C. Marshall* (New York: Viking Penguin, 1987), 4:40.
3. *Ibid.*, 60.
4. *Ibid.*, 3.
5. *Ibid.*, 4.
6. Thomas Parrish, *Roosevelt and Marshall: Partners in Politics and War* (New York: William Morrow, 1989), 37–38.
7. *Ibid.*, x.
8. Pogue, *George C. Marshall*, 4:70.
9. *Ibid.*, 4:76.
10. *Ibid.*, 4:xi.
11. *Ibid.*, 4:142.
12. *Ibid.*, 4:515.
13. *Ibid.*, 2:41.
14. *Ibid.*, 4:431.
15. *Ibid.*, 4:491.
16. *Ibid.*, 4:515.
17. Rushworth Kidder, *How Good People Make Tough Choices* (New York: Harper, 1995), 110.
18. *Ibid.*, 6.
19. Rushworth Kidder, *Moral Courage* (New York: William Morrow, 2005),106.
20. *Ibid.*, 10.
21. François Wisard, "Context and Milestones of the Rescue Activities of Carl Lutz and His Team," in *Under Swiss Protection: Jewish Eyewitness Accounts from Wartime Budapest*, ed. A. Hirschi and C. Schallie (Stuttgart: Ibidem-Verlag, 2017), 40.
22. *Ibid.*, 48.
23. *Ibid.*, 33–34.
24. *Ibid.*, 36–38.
25. *Ibid.*, 41
26. *Ibid.*, 44.
27. *Ibid.*, 34.
28. *Ibid.*, 34–35.
29. *Ibid.*, 44–45. Wisard for some reason sets the figure at 7,000. The standard figure is 8,000.
30. Paul Fabry, "Carl Lutz Stood Out like a Monument—He Was an Example of What Can Be Done," in *Under Swiss Protection: Jewish Eyewitness Accounts from Wartime Budapest*, ed. A. Hirschi and C. Schallie (Stuttgart: Ibidem-Verlag, 2017), 59.
31. Wisard, "Context and Milestone," 46.
32. *Ibid.*, 46–47.
33. *Ibid.*, 47.
34. *Ibid.*, 39–40.
35. Theo Tschuy, *Dangerous Diplomacy: The Story of Carl Lutz, Rescuer of 62,000 Hungarian Jews* (Grand Rapids: Eerdmans, 2000), xi.
36. Wisard, "Context and Milestone," 44.
37. Fabry, "Carl Lutz," 55.
38. Doris Kearns Goodwin, *Team of Rivals: The Political Genius of Abraham*

Lincoln (New York: Simon & Schuster, 2006), 470–471.

39. As cited in Stephen Covey, *The 8th Habit: From Effectiveness to Greatness* (New York: Free Press, 2004), 81.

40. Kevin Dougherty, *Encyclopedia of the Confederacy* (San Diego: Thunder Bay Press, 2010), 72.

41. *Ibid.*

42. *Ibid.*, 104–105.

43. Goodwin, *Team of Rivals*, 470–471; emphasis in original.

44. *Ibid.*, 470–471.

45. M.K. Gandhi, *Statement to Disorders Inquiry Committee* (Calcutta: Superintendent Government Printing, India, 1920).

46. *Ibid.*

47. T.C. Schelling, "Egonomics, or the Art of Self-Management," *American Economic Review* 68, no. 2 (May 1978): 291.

48. *Ibid.*, 290. The decision of conquistador Hernán Cortés in 1519 to burn his ships to prevent the faint-hearted from abandoning his expedition in Mexico and fleeing to Cuba is an oft-cited example of precommitment.

49. Stephen Covey, *The 7 Habits of Highly Effective People* (New York: Simon & Schuster, 1989), 83.

50. Ramachandra Guha, *Gandhi: The Years that Changed the World; 1914–1948* (New York: Knopf, 2018), 4–5.

51. M.K. Gandhi, *An Autobiography or the Story of My Experiments with Truth: A Critical Edition* (New Haven: Yale University Press, 2018), 230–231.

52. *Ibid.*, 499.

53. *Ibid.*

54. *Ibid.*, 499–500.

55. Talat Ahmed, *Mohandas Gandhi: Experiments in Civil Disobedience* (Las Vegas: Pluto Press, 2019), 38–41.

56. *Ibid.*, 30.

57. Gandhi, *Autobiography*, 500.

58. Guha, *Gandhi*, 318.

59. *Ibid.*, 320.

60. Rachel Fell McDermott et al., *Sources of Indian Traditions: Modern India, Pakistan, and Bangladesh* (New York: University of Columbia Press, 2014), 367–369.

61. Guha, *Gandhi*, 331.

62. *Ibid.*, 333–334.

63. *Ibid.*, 338.

64. James Martin, *Justice Ignited: The Dynamics of Backfire* (Lantham, MD: Rowan & Littlefield, 2007), 38.

65. Guha, *Gandhi*, 355.

66. Ahmed, *Mohandas Gandhi*, 105–107.

67. "Years of Arrests and Imprisonments of Mahatma Gandhi," Available at mkgandhi.org.

68. Gandhi, *Autobiography*, 769.

69. Gandhi, *Statement to Disorders Inquiry Committee.*

Military Leaders

1. "Executive Order 10631—Code of Conduct for Members of the Armed Forces of the United States," National Archives, https://www.archives.gov/federal-register/codification/executive-order/10631.html.

2. *Ibid.*

3. *The U.S. Fighting Man's Code* (Washington, D.C.: Office of Armed Forces Information and Education, Department of Defense, 1955), 42–44.

4. John McCain, "John McCain, Prisoner of War: A First-Person Account," *U.S. News & World Report*, January 28, 2008, https://www.usnews.com/news/articles/2008/01/28/john-mccain-prisoner-of-war-a-first-person-account.

5. John McCain, *Faith of My Fathers* (New York: Random House, 1999), 238.

6. "Executive Order 10631."

7. *The U.S. Fighting Man's Code*, 42.

8. McCain, "Prisoner of War."

9. James Sterba, "POW Commander among 108 Freed," *New York Times*, March 15, 1973.

10. Stephen Covey, *Principled-Centered Leadership* (New York: Fireside, 1992), 46–49.

11. Ryan Gibb, "The Elections in Uganda, February 2016," *African Spectrum* 51, no. 2 (2016), https://journals.sagepub.com/doi/10.1177/000203971605100206.

12. Institutional Crisis Group,

"Uganda's Slow Slide into Crisis," *Africa Report*, November 21, 2017, 1.

13. Sam Wilkins and Richard Vokes, *Elections in Museveni's Uganda: Understanding the 2016 Polls* (New York: Routledge, 2018), 1.

14. Paul Nantulya, "Wisdom from Africa on Ethical Leadership," Africa Center for Strategic Studies, May 9, 2017. https://africacenter.org/spotlight/wisdom-africa-ethical-leadership/ and Gibb.

15. "Army to Preserve Peace, Not Shoot People—Says Katumba," *Monitor*, January 26, 2021, https://www.monitor.co.ug/uganda/news/national/army-to-preserve-peace-not-shoot-people-says-katumba-1639486.

16. "International Hall of Fame Inducts General Edward Katumba Wamala," U.S. Army War College Archives, September 18, 2014, https://www.armywarcollege.edu/News/archives/12425.pdf; "Six UPDF Generals Receive U.S. Legion of Merit Award," U.S. Embassy in Uganda, September 30, 2015, https://ug.usembassy.gov/six-updf-generals-receive-u-s-legion-of-merit-award/.

17. "Katumba Wamala Shooting: Uganda Minister's Daughter Killed," BBC, June 1, 2021, https://www.bbc.com/news/world-africa-57315083.

18. Nantulya, "Wisdom."

19. *Ibid.*

20. "Uganda Polls: Museveni's Main Rival, Besigye, Arrested," BBC News, February 19, 2016, https://www.bbc.com/news/world-africa-35612224.

21. Nantulya, "Wisdom."

22. James Kouzes and Barry Posner, *The Leadership Challenge: How to Make Extraordinary Things Happen in Organizations*, 5th ed. (New York: Wiley, 2012), 68.

23. Nantulya, "Wisdom."

24. Robert Coram, *Boyd: The Fighter Pilot Who Changed the Art of War* (Boston: Little, Brown, 2002).

25. Ian Brown, *A New Conception of War: John Boyd, the U.S. Marines, and Maneuver Warfare* (Quantico, VA: Marine Corps University Press, 2018), 14–15.

26. Jacob Neufeld, *The F-15 Eagle: Origins and Development, 1964–1972* (Washington, D.C.: Office of Air Force History, 1974), 18.

27. Brown, *New Conception*, 17.

28. *Ibid.*

29. *Ibid.*, 17–18.

30. Neufeld, *F-15 Eagle*, 18.

31. Brown, *New Conception*, 19.

32. *Ibid.*

33. Marshall Michel, "The Revolt of the Majors: How the Air Force Changed after Vietnam" (PhD diss., Auburn University, 2006), 103.

34. *Ibid.*, 81–83.

35. Brown, *New Conception*, 20–21.

36. *Ibid.*, 28–29.

37. Coram, *Boyd*, 7.

38. Michel, "Revolt of the Majors," 81. Michel references Timothy Lefler's description of "critics" as members of a group that have support neither for their proposals nor an interest in succeeding by conciliation and cooperation, and "reformers" as one who can "bridge the gap between criticism and successful reform by recognizing the obstacles to change, and then gaining the support of state authority and the cooperation of the active participants." Boyd and Sprey, Michel argues "were never interested in bridging the gap and becoming reformers; they preferred to remain critics."

39. Coram, *Boyd*, 8.

40. Anthony DeLellis, "Clarifying the Concept of Respect: Implications for Leadership," *Journal of Leadership Studies* 7, no. 2 (2000): 44.

41. Michael Bilton and Kevin Sim, *Four Hours in My Lai* (New York: Penguin Books, 1993), 109.

42. Trent Angers, *The Forgotten Hero of My Lai: The Hugh Thompson Story* (Lafayette, LA: Acadian House, 2014), 234.

43. *Ibid.*, 74–76.

44. Bilton and Sim, *Four Hours*, 135.

45. Angers, *Forgotten Hero*, 76–77.

46. *Ibid.*, 78–80.

47. *Ibid.*, 80–83.

48. *Ibid.*, 83–87.
49. *Ibid.*, 88.
50. "Witness Says He Didn't Report Mylai Civilian Deaths to Medina," *New York Times*, August 21, 1971, 9, https://www.nytimes.com/1971/08/21/archives/witness-says-he-didnt-report-mylai-civilian-deaths-to-medina.html.
51. Bilton and Sims, *Four Hours*, 109.
52. *Ibid.*, 128.
53. *Ibid.*, 134.
54. *Ibid.*, 146.
55. *Report of the Department of the Army Review of the Preliminary Investigation into the My Lai Incident* (Washington, D.C.: Department of the Army, March 14, 1970), 12–1.
56. *Ibid.*, 12–2.
57. *Ibid.*, 12–3.
58. Howard Jones, *My Lai: Vietnam, 1968, and the Descent into Darkness* (Oxford: Oxford University Press, 2017), 286.
59. Angers, *Forgotten Hero*, 94.
60. Rick Rubel and George Lucas, *Case Studies in Ethics for Military Leaders* (Boston: Pearson, 2015), 223.
61. Angers, *Forgotten Hero*, 160.
62. *Ibid.*, 155–182.
63. *Ibid.*, 177–178.
64. "My Lai Rescuer Hugh Thompson Jr.," *Washington Post*, January 7, 2016, https://www.washingtonpost.com/archive/local/2006/01/07/my-lai-rescuer-hugh-thompson-jr/29df090b-c47a-4a9c-af0f-6b453ec907bd/.

Religious Leaders

1. *The Holy Bible*, NIV, Daniel 1:3.
2. Daniel 1:4–5.
3. Daniel 1:8–16.
4. Daniel 1:10.
5. Daniel 3:5–6.
6. Daniel 3:13–18.
7. Stephen Covey, *The 8th Habit: From Effectiveness to Greatness* (New York: Free Press, 2004), 46–49.
8. Daniel 3:28.
9. Daniel 6:3.
10. Daniel 6:4–5.
11. Daniel 6:7.
12. Daniel 6:10.
13. Daniel 6:21.
14. Daniel 6:26.
15. Quoted in William Safire, "On Language: Principles vs Values," *New York Times*, August 12, 1984, section 6, 8.
16. Daniel 6:10.
17. International Buddhist Information Bureau, "Thich Quang Do Is Appointed New Leader of the Unified Buddhist Church of Vietnam," August 17, 2008, https://www.europarl.europa.eu/meetdocs/2004_2009/documents/dv/droi_080825_thichquangdo/DROI_080825_ThichQuangDoen.pdf.
18. James O'Toole, "Speaking Truth to Power: A White Paper," Markkula Center for Applied Ethics, https://www.scu.edu/ethics/focus-areas/business-ethics/resources/speaking-truth-to-power-a-white-paper/.
19. *Ibid.*
20. Amy Davidson Sorkin, "Madame Nhu's Match," *New Yorker*, April 26, 2011, https://www.newyorker.com/news/amy-davidson/madame-nhus-match.
21. "Vietnam," United States Center for International Religious Freedom, https://www.uscirf.gov/sites/default/files/Vietnam.pdf.
22. "Thich Quang Do, Vietnam Dissident Buddhist Monk, Dies at 91," *Washington Post*, February 25, 2020, https://www.washingtonpost.com/local/obituaries/thich-quang-do-vietnam-dissident-buddhist-monk-dies-at-91/2020/02/25/e179c012-5806-11ea-ab68-101ecfec2532_story.html.
23. International Buddhist Information Bureau, "Thich Quang Do."
24. Rafto Prize, "Laureate 2006: Thich Quang Do; Peaceful Opposition against the Communist Regime," https://www.rafto.no/en/the-rafto-prize/thich-quang-do.
25. Unified Buddhist Church of Vietnam, "An Appeal for Democracy in Vietnam," February 21, 2001, http://danchuqueme.free.fr/document/e-keugoi.htm. See also *Journal of Democracy* 27, no. 3 (July 2016): 186–187.

26. Rafto Prize, "Laureate 2006."

27. International Buddhist Information Bureau, "Thich Quang Do."

28. Seth Mydans, "Thich Quang Do, 91, Buddhist Monk and Rights Champion in Vietnam," *New York Times,* February 27, 2020.

29. "Thich Quang Do."

30. International Buddhist Information Bureau, "Thich Quang Do."

31. Mydans, "Thich Quang Do, 91."

32. International Buddhist Information Bureau, "Thich Quang Do."

33. Mydans, "Thich Quang Do, 91."

34. Jan de Volder, *The Spirit of Father Damien: The Leper Priest—a Saint for Our Time* (San Francisco: Ignatius Press, 2010), 39.

35. James Hunter, *The Servant: A Simple Story about the True Essence of Leadership* (New York: Crown Currency, 1998), 125.

36. Karen Hendrikz and Amos Engelbrecht, "The Principled Leadership Scale: An Integration of Value-Based Leadership," *SA Journal of Industrial Psychology* 45 (March 2019): 2.

37. Robert Greenleaf, *Servant Leadership: A Journey into the Nature of Legitimate Power & Greatness* (New York: Paulist Press, 2002), 6.

38. Stephen Covey, *Principle-Centered Leadership* (New York: Simon & Schuster, 1992), 34.

39. John Farrow, *Damien the Leper* (New York: Sheed & Ward, 1937), 73.

40. Kalaupapa National Park, "A Brief History of Kalaupapa," https://www.nps.gov/kala/learn/historyculture/a-brief-history-of-kalaupapa.htm.

41. Farrow, *Damien the Leper,* 75.

42. *Ibid.,* 80–81.

43. Sen Sendjaya, James C. Sarros, and Joseph C. Santora, "Defining and Measuring Servant Leadership Behaviour in Organizations," *Journal of Management Studies* 45, no. 2 (March 2008): 406.

44. Farrow, *Damien the Leper,* 81.

45. *Ibid.,* 82.

46. De Volder, *Spirit of Father Damien,* 39.

47. Farrow, *Damien the Leper,* 84.

48. *Ibid.,* 99.

49. *Ibid.,* 101.

50. *Ibid.,* 100.

51. *Ibid.,* 101–102.

52. *Ibid.,* 103.

53. *Ibid.,* 110.

54. *Ibid.,* 114.

55. *Ibid.,* 115–116.

56. *Ibid.,* 107.

57. *Ibid.,* 105–106.

58. *Ibid.,* 107.

59. *Ibid.,* 106.

60. *Ibid.,* 107.

61. *Ibid.,* 116.

62. Michael Davis, "The Meaning of Father Damien," *Crisis Magazine,* August 3, 2020, https://www.crisismagazine.com/2020/the-meaning-of-father-damien.

63. De Volder, *Spirit of Father Damien,* x.

64. Rachel Donadio, "Benedict Canonizes 5 New Saints," *New York Times,* October 11, 2009.

65. Acts 15:17.

66. Galatians 2:11–14

67. Acts 15:1–2.

68. Manuel London, "Principled Leadership and Business Diplomacy: A Practical, Values-Based Direction for Management Development," *Journal of Management Development* 18, no. 2 (1999): 174.

69. *Ibid.,* 175.

70. Stanley Porter, "Conflict Resolution: Leadership and the Jerusalem Council," in *Biblical Leadership: Theology for the Everyday Leader,* ed. Benjamin Forrest and Chet Roden (Grand Rapids: Kregel, 2017), 396–397.

71. Frank Cross and Elizabeth Livingstone, eds., *The Oxford Dictionary of the Christian Church,* 3rd rev. ed. (Oxford: Oxford University Press, 2005), 912.

72. T.C. Smith, *The Broadman Bible Commentary, vol. 10, Acts–1 Corinthians* (Nashville: Broadman, 1970), 90.

73. Porter, "Conflict Resolution," 399, 401.

74. Acts 15:13.

75. Porter, "Conflict Resolution," 399.

76. Smith, *Broadman Bible Commentary,* 90.

77. Porter, "Conflict Resolution," 403–404.

78. Acts 15:15.

79. Porter, "Conflict Resolution," 406.

80. Acts 15:19–20.

81. Porter, "Conflict Resolution," 404.

82. Step 2 of Glynn and Jamerson's three-step process of principled leadership is "self-reflection on one's personal values, the firm's values, and their alignment." Maryann Glynn and Heather Jamerson, "Principled Leadership: A Framework for Action," in *Leading with Values: Positivity, Virtue and High Performance*, ed. E.D. Hess and K.S. Cameron (Cambridge: Cambridge University Press, 2006), 164–165.

83. James Kouzes and Barry Posner write that options contrary to the leader's core values "are seldom considered or acted on; and if they are, it's done with a sense of compliance rather than commitment." James Kouzes and Barry Posner, *The Leadership Challenge: How to Make Extraordinary Things Happen in Organizations*, 5th ed. (New York: Wiley, 2012), 49.

84. Acts 15:23.

85. Acts 15:28–29.

86. Porter, "Conflict Resolution," 404.

87. Amos 15:21.

88. Anna Simons, "Backbone vs. Box: The Choice between Principled and Prescriptive Leadership," in *The Future of the Army Profession*, ed. L. Matthews (New York: McGraw-Hill, 2002), 379.

89. Carrie Menkel-Meadow, "Ethics of Compromise," in *Global Encyclopedia of Public Administration, Public Policy, and Governance*, ed. Ali Farazmand (Basel: Springer, 2016), https://www.law.uci.edu/faculty/full-time/menkel-meadow/ethics-as-compromise-Ency.of-Public-Admin-and-Policy.pdf.

Sports Leaders

1. Edward Shillito, "British Table Talk," *Christian Century* 40, no. 51 (December 21, 1923): 1660.

2. James Kouzes and Barry Posner write that options contrary to the leader's core values "are seldom considered or acted on; and if they are, it's done with a sense of compliance rather than commitment." James Kouzes and Barry Posner, *The Leadership Challenge: How to Make Extraordinary Things Happen in Organizations*, 5th ed. (New York: Wiley, 2012), 49.

3. Julian Wilson, *Complete Surrender: A Biography of Eric Liddell* (Bletchley, UK: Authentic Media, 2012).

4. Shillito, 1660.

5. Eric Mataxas, *Seven Men: And the Secret of Their Greatness* (Nashville: Thomas Nelson, 2016), 86.

6. Wilson, *Complete Surrender.*

7. Mataxas, *Seven Men*, 66–67.

8. *Ibid.*, 68.

9. *Ibid.*, 71.

10. *Ibid.*, 70.

11. *Ibid.*, 65.

12. Eric Eichinger, *The Final Race: The Incredible World War II Story of the Olympian Who Inspired* Chariots of Fire (Colorado Springs: NavPress, 2018).

13. Mataxas, *Seven Men*, 85.

14. Wilson, *Complete Surrender.*

15. Michael Schoenecke, "Bobby Jones, Golf, and His Instructional Reels," *Film & History* 35, no. 2 (2005): 68.

16. Alistair Cooke, *Alistair Cooke's America* (London: Orion, 2003).

17. Schoenecke, "Bobby Jones," 68.

18. Stephen Lowe, *"The Greatest Ever" and a Return to Merion, 1924–1925. Sir Walter and Mr. Jones: Walter Hagen, Bobby Jones, and the Rise of American Golf* (Ann Arbor: Sleeping Bear Press, 2000), 253.

19. Michael Bohn, *Heroes & Ballyhoo: How the Golden Age of the 1920s Transformed American Sports* (Sterling, VA: Potomac Books, 2009), 282; Schoenecke, "Bobby Jones," 68.

20. Schoenecke, "Bobby Jones," 68.

21. Bohn, *Heroes & Ballyhoo*, 3.

22. Charles Reagan Wilson, "Bobby Jones," in *The New Encyclopedia of Southern Culture*, vol. 16, *Sports and Recreation*, ed. Harvey H. Jackson, III (Chapel Hill: University of North Carolina Press, 2011), 309.

23. *Ibid.*
24. *Ibid.*
25. *Ibid.*
26. Bobby Jones, *Golf Is My Game* (New York: Doubleday, 1960), 172–173.
27. Wilson, "Bobby Jones," 309.
28. https://www.usga.org/content/usga/home-page/about/usga-bob-jones-award.html
29. Gene Klann, *The Application of Power and Influence in Organizational Leadership* (Fort Leavenworth, KS: CGSC, 2010), 2.
30. Schoenecke, "Bobby Jones," 68.
31. Bill Fields, "Golf's Renaissance Legend, Bobby Jones," The Masters, October 21, 2020, https://www.masters.com/en_US/news/articles/2020-10-21/2020-10-21_golfs_renaissance_legend_bobby_jones.html.
32. Armando Galarraga, Jim Joyce, and Daniel Paisner, *Nobody's Perfect: Two Men, One Call, and a Game for Baseball History* (New York: Atlantic Monthly Press, 2011), 12.
33. Tony Paul, "10 Years Later, Ex-Tiger Armando Galarraga 'Lucky to Not Be Lucky' in Brush with Perfection," *Detroit News*, June 1, 2020.
34. *Ibid.*
35. *Ibid.*
36. *Ibid.*
37. *Ibid.*
38. Thomas Boswell, "The Game Wasn't Perfect, but the Gentlemen Were," *Washington Post*, June 4, 2010, A01.
39. Susan Tish, "A Pitcher, an Umpire, and a Lesson in Grace," *Christian Science Monitor*, June 9, 2010.
40. Paul, "10 Years Later."
41. *Ibid.*
42. *Ibid.*
43. *Ibid.*
44. Galarraga et al., *Nobody's Perfect*, 12.
45. "Read Rachael Denhollander's Full Victim Impact Statement about Larry Nassar," CNN, January 30, 2018, https://www.cnn.com/2018/01/24/us/rachael-denhollander-full-statement/index.html. All subsequent references to the impact statement are from this source.
46. Lynn Paine, "Managing for Organizational Integrity," *Harvard Business Review*, March 1, 1994, 115.
47. Stephen Covey, *The 8th Habit: From Effectiveness to Greatness* (New York: Free Press, 2004), 49.
48. Joseph Badaracco, *Questions of Character: Illuminating the Heart of Leadership through Literature* (Boston: Harvard Business Review Press, 2006), 55.
49. James Kouzes and Barry Posner, *The Leadership Challenge: How to Make Extraordinary Things Happen in Organizations*, 5th ed. (New York: Wiley, 2012), 16; Covey, *The 8th Habit*, 5.

Literary Characters

1. Harper Lee, *To Kill a Mockingbird* (Philadelphia: Lippincott, 1960), 36.
2. *Ibid.*, 26–27.
3. *Ibid.*, 28.
4. *Ibid.*, 36.
5. *Ibid.*, 215–216.
6. *Ibid.*, 209, 216.
7. *Ibid.*, 212–213.
8. *Ibid.*, 213–214.
9. *Ibid.*, 215, 218.
10. *Ibid.*, 248–249.
11. *Ibid.*, 255.
12. *Ibid.*, 290.
13. *Ibid.*, 292–294.
14. *Ibid.*, 295–296.
15. Quoted in Edgar Puryear, *American Generalship: Character Is Everything; the Art of Command* (Novato, CA: Presidio, 2000), 188.
16. Kenny Williams, "*Adventures of Huckleberry Finn*; or, Mark Twain's Racial Ambiguity," in *Satire or Evasion: Black Perspectives on* Huckleberry Finn, ed. James Leonard, Thomas Tenney, and Thadious Davis (Durham, NC: Duke University Press, 1992), 234.
17. Mark Twain, *Adventures of Huckleberry Finn* (New York: Charles L. Webster, 1885), 32.
18. *Ibid.*, 33.
19. *Ibid.*, 1–2.

20. *Ibid.*, 59–60.
21. *Ibid.*, 69.
22. *Ibid.*, 405.
23. *Ibid.*, 89.
24. *Ibid.*, 162.
25. Betty Jones, "Huck and Jim: A Reconsideration," in *Satire or Evasion: Black Perspectives on* Huckleberry Finn, ed. James Leonard, Thomas Tenney, and Thadious Davis (Durham, NC: Duke University Press, 1992), 157.
26. Twain, *Huckleberry Finn*, 296.
27. *Ibid.*, 112.
28. *Ibid.*, 116–118.
29. *Ibid.*, 119.
30. *Ibid.*, 120.
31. Jones, "Huck and Jim," 156.
32. Jocelyn Chadwick-Joshua, *The Jim Dilemma: Reading Race in* Huckleberry Finn (Oxford: University Press of Mississippi, 1998), xii.
33. Twain, *Huckleberry Finn*, 123.
34. *Ibid.*, 124–125.
35. *Ibid.*, 381.
36. *Ibid.*, 304–305.
37. Jones, "Huck and Jim," 163.
38. Williams, "Adventures of Huckleberry Finn," 233.
39. Twain, *Huckleberry Finn*, 405.
40. Samuel Huntington, *The Soldier and the State: The Theory and Politics of Civil-Military Relations* (Cambridge, MA: Belknap, 1959), 72.
41. *Ibid.*, 79.
42. *Ibid.*, 83–84.
43. "Farewell Address," Dwight D. Eisenhower Presidential Library, https://www.eisenhowerlibrary.gov/sites/default/files/research/online-documents/farewell-address/reading-copy.pdf.
44. Gerald Pratley, *The Cinema of John Frankenheimer* (New York: Zwemmer/Barnes, 1969), 113.
45. Hal Erikson, *Any Resemblance to Actual Persons: The Real People behind 400+ Fictional Movie Characters* (Jefferson, NC: McFarland, 2017), 352.
46. Robert Dalleck, "JFK vs. the Military," *The Atlantic*, August 2013, https://www.theatlantic.com/magazine/archive/2013/08/jfk-vs-the-military/309496/.
47. Michael Coyne, *Hollywood Goes to Washington: American Politics on Screen* (London: Reaktion Books, 2008), 153.
48. John Gardner, *On Leadership* (New York: Free Press, 1990), 191.
49. *Ibid.*
50. Irving Janis, *Groupthink: Psychological Studies of Policy Decisions and Fiascoes* (Boston: Houghton Mifflin, 1982), 9.
51. Joshua Goldstein and Jon Pevehouse, *International Relations* (New York: Longman, 2010), 111.
52. Steven Hook, *U.S. Foreign Policy: The Paradox of World Power*, 2nd ed. (Washington, DC: CQ Press, 2007), 92.
53. Janis, *Groupthink*, 9–10.
54. Gardner, *On Leadership*, 191.

Societal Leaders

1. Rosa Parks, *Rosa Parks: My Story* (New York: Puffin, 1999), 110.
2. *Ibid.*, 46–49.
3. *Journal of the Proceedings of the Constitutional Convention of the State of Alabama, Held in the City of Montgomery, Commencing May 21st, 1901* (Montgomery, AL: Brown Printing, 1901), 9.
4. "Rosa Parks: In Her Own Words," https://www.loc.gov/exhibitions/rosa-parks-in-her-own-words/about-this-exhibition/a-life-of-global-impact/.
5. Douglas Brinkley, *Rosa Parks: A Life* (New York: Penguin, 2005), 105–107.
6. *Ibid.*, 108.
7. Margot Adler, "Before Rosa Parks, There Was Claudette Colvin," NPR, March 15, 2009, https://www.npr.org/2009/03/15/101719889/before-rosa-parks-there-was-claudette-colvin.
8. Brinkley, *Rosa Parks*, 116.
9. Taylor Branch, *Parting of the Waters America in the King Years 1954–63* (New York: Simon & Schuster, 1989), 130.
10. Brinkley, *Rosa Parks*, 116.
11. Jo Ann Gibson Robinson, *Montgomery Bus Boycott and the Women Who Started It: The Memoir of Jo Ann Gibson Robinson* (Knoxville: University of Tennessee Press, 1987), 45–46.
12. Brinkley, *Rosa Parks*, 170.
13. David Lightner, *Asylum, Prison,*

and Poorhouse: The Writings and Reform Work of Dorothea Dix in Illinois (Carbondale: Southern Illinois University Press, 1999), 29.

14. *Ibid.* The verse is found in Matthew 7:12.

15. Manon Perry, "Dorothea Dix (1802–1887)," *American Journal of Public Health* 96, no. 4 (April 2006): 624–625; Frank B. Norbury, "Dorothea Dix and the Founding of Illinois' First Mental Hospital," *Journal of the Illinois State Historical Society* 92, no. 1 (Spring 1999): 15.

16. Norbury, "Dorothea Dix," 15–16.

17. *Ibid.*, 16.

18. Markkula Center for Applied Ethics at Santa Clara University, "A Framework for Ethical Decision Making," https://www.scu.edu/ethics/ethics-resources/ethical-decision-making/a-framework-for-ethical-decision-making/. Glynn and Jamerson write that "as an initial step, leaders must become aware of the moral and ethical dimensions of a particular situation, and evaluate the extent to which the existing conceptual models attend to these moral and ethical issues." Maryann Glynn and Heather Jamerson, "Principled Leadership: A Framework for Action," in *Leading with Values: Positivity, Virtue and High Performance*, ed. E.D. Hess and K.S. Cameron (Cambridge: Cambridge University Press, 2006), 165.

19. Lightner, *Asylum, Prison, and Poorhouse*, 4–5.

20. *Ibid.*, 5–6.

21. Norbury, "Dorothea Dix," 19–20.

22. Lightner, *Asylum, Prison, and Poorhouse*, 14; emphasis in original..

23. William Safire, "On Language: Principles vs Values," *New York Times*, August 12, 1984, section 6, 8.

24. Stephen Covey, *The 8th Habit: From Effectiveness to Greatness* (New York: Free Press, 2004), 46–49.

25. James Kouzes and Barry Posner write that options contrary to the leader's core values "are seldom considered or acted on; and if they are, it's done with a sense of compliance rather than commitment." James Kouzes and Barry Posner, *The Leadership Challenge: How to Make Extraordinary Things Happen in Organizations*, 5th ed. (New York: Wiley, 2012), 49.

26. Lightner, *Asylum, Prison, and Poorhouse*, 29.

27. Badaracco argues that "combining principles and pragmatism is among the most difficult challenges leaders face." Joseph Badaracco, *Questions of Character: Illuminating the Heart of Leadership through Literature* (Boston: Harvard Business Review Press, 2006), 140.

28. Lightner, *Asylum, Prison, and Poorhouse*, 13, 16.

29. *Ibid.*, 29–30.

30. *Ibid.*, 103–104.

31. *Ibid.*, 106–109.

32. *Ibid.*, 109.

33. *Ibid.*, 120.

34. *Ibid.*, 102, 7.

35. Step 2 of Glynn and Jamerson's three-step process of principled leadership process is "self-reflection on one's personal values, the firm's values, and their alignment." Step 1 is "awareness, making moral and ethical dimensions an explicit part of leadership decisions and action." Glynn and Jamerson, "Principled Leadership," 164–165.

36. James Kouzes and Barry Posner write that options contrary to the leader's core values "are seldom considered or acted on; and if they are, it's done with a sense of compliance rather than commitment." Kouzes and Posner, *The Leadership Challenge*, 49.

37. Isaac Prilleltensky notes that one risk faced by value-based leaders is "to remain at a level of abstraction that makes for an internally coherent set of values but that is of little use in practice. Values have to be articulated in such a way that they can be translated into concrete policies and guidelines." Isaac Prilleltensky, "Value-Based Leadership in Organizations: Balancing Values, Interests, and Power among Citizens, Workers, and Leaders," *Ethics & Behavior* 10, no. 2 (2000): 151.

38. Badaracco argues that "combining principles and pragmatism is among

the most difficult challenges leaders face." Badaracco, *Questions of Character*, 140.

39. Joi-Marie MacKenzie, "High School Senior Creates Group 'We Dine Together' So No Student Has to Eat Alone," ABC News, March 16, 2017, https://abcnews.go.com/Lifestyle/high-school-senior-creates-group-dine-student-eat/story?id=46172969.

40. Alanna Quillen, "Boca Lunch Club's Mission That No Kid Should Alone Goes Viral," WPTV, March 28, 2017, https://www.wptv.com/news/region-s-palm-beach-county/boca-raton/boca-lunch-clubs-mission-that-no-kid-should-alone-goes-viral.

41. Caitlin McGlade, "Eating Alone at School: How Four Students Began Mission to End Isolation," *Sun Sentinel*, February 18, 2017, https://www.sun-sentinel.com/news/education/fl-eating-alone-at-school-20170205-story.html.

42. McGlade, "Eating Alone at School."

43. MacKenzie, "High School Senior."

44. McGlade, "Eating Alone at School."

45. Robert Weich, "Florida High Schooler Ensures Everyone Has Someone to Sit with at Lunch," CBS58, November 25, 2017, https://www.cbs58.com/news/florida-high-schooler-ensures-everyone-has-someone-to-sit-with-at-lunch.

46. "Denis Estimon, CEO of We Dine Together, Steps in as New Director of Be Strong," Be Strong, https://bestrong.global/tag/denis-estimon/.

47. Peter Northouse, *Leadership: Theory and Practice*, 8th ed. (Thousand Oaks: Sage, 2019), 8.

48. Bob Johansen, *Leaders Make the Future: Ten New Leadership Skills for an Uncertain World* (Oakland, CA: Berrett-Koehler, 2009), 20.

49. As argued previously, principles, not values, are the operative element of "principled" leadership, but as John Gardner explains, "if leaders cannot find in their constituencies any base of shared values, principled leadership becomes nearly impossible." John Gardner, *On Leadership* (New York: Free Press, 1990), 113.

50. James Kouzes and Barry Posner, *The Leadership Challenge* (San Francisco: Jossey-Bass, 2012), 209.

51. Northouse, *Leadership*, 10.

52. Cathy Free, "Florida High School Students Start Lunch Club So No One Eats Alone: 'Relationships Are Built from across the Table,'" *People*, April 7, 2017, https://people.com/human-interest/florida-high-school-students-start-lunch-club-no-one-eats-alone/.

53. *Ibid.*

54. Marcus Luttrell describes the decision-making process employed by the SEALs as they pondered what to do with the goatherders in Marcus Luttrell with Patrick Robinson, *Lone Survivor*, large print ed. (Farmington Hills, MI: Thorndike Press, 2007), 301–311. It is an interesting comparison and contrast with the process of principled leadership described in the Introduction of this book.

55. *Ibid.*, 458.

56. *Ibid.*, 423.

57. Patrick Robinson, *Lion of Sabray*, Kindle ed. (New York: Touchstone, 2016).

58. *Ibid.*

59. Luttrell, *Lone Survivor*, 425.

60. *Ibid.*, 432–443.

61. *Ibid.*, 444–450.

62. *Ibid.*, 455.

63. *Ibid.*, 461.

64. *Ibid.*, 456.

65. *Ibid.*, 463–473

66. *Ibid.*, 474.

67. *Ibid.*, 502.

68. *Ibid.*, 506–507.

69. Luttrell refers to Shah by the code name "Ben Sharmak" in *Lone Survivor*.

70. *Ibid.*, 513–516.

71. *Ibid.*, 518.

72. *Ibid.*, 529.

73. Robinson, *Lion of Sabray*.

74. X. Jasmine Bordere and Franklin Mixon, "Did Servant-Leadership Save the Lone Survivor? The Pashtunwali Ethos as a Foundation for the Practice of Servant Leadership," *International Journal*

of Servant Leadership 14, no. 1 (2020): 370, 378–379.

Conclusion

1. Karen Hendrikz and Amos Engelbrecht, "The Principled Leadership Scale: An Integration of Value-Based Leadership," *SA Journal of Industrial Psychology* 45 (March 2019): 2.

2. Stanley Porter, "Conflict Resolution: Leadership and the Jerusalem Council," in *Biblical Leadership: Theology for the Everyday Leader*, ed. Benjamin Forrest and Chet Roden (Grand Rapids: Kregel, 2017), 404.

3. Anna Simons, "Backbone vs. Box: The Choice between Principled and Prescriptive Leadership," in *The Future of the Army Profession*, ed. L. Matthews (New York: McGraw-Hill, 2002), 379.

4. Marshall Goldsmith, *What Got You Here Won't Get You There: How Successful People Become Even More Successful* (New York: Hyperion, 2007), 207–208.

5. *The Guidon* (Charleston, SC: The Citadel, 2021), 109; emphasis added.

6. Augustine of Hippo; Sermon 110 on 1 John 4:4–12, para. 8.

Appendix 1

1. CADRE, http://www.cadre-la.org/core/about/beliefs-values-principles/. Reproduced here by permission of CADRE.

Bibliography

Adler, Margot. "Before Rosa Parks, There Was Claudette Colvin." NPR, March 15, 2009. https://www.npr.org/2009/03/15/101719889/before-rosa-parks-there-was-claudette-colvin.

Ahmed, Talat. *Mohandas Gandhi: Experiments in Civil Disobedience.* Las Vegas: Pluto Press, 2019.

Angers, Trent. *The Forgotten Hero of My Lai: The Hugh Thompson Story.* Lafayette, LA: Acadian House, 2014.

"Army to Preserve Peace, Not Shoot People—Says Katumba." *Monitor,* January 26, 2021. https://www.monitor.co.ug/uganda/news/national/army-to-preserve-peace-not-shoot-people-says-katumba-1639486.

"Ashland Accepts Oil Spill Accord." *New York Times,* September 9, 1989. https://www.nytimes.com/1989/11/09/us/ashland-accepts-oil-spill-accord.html.

Badaracco, Joseph. *Questions of Character: Illuminating the Heart of Leadership through Literature.* Boston: Harvard Business Review Press, 2006.

Bernheim, Ruth, and Alan Melnick. "Principled Leadership in Public Health: Integrating Ethics into Practice and Management." *Journal of Public Health Management & Practice* 14, no. 4 (July/August 2008): 358–66.

Bilton, Michael, and Kevin Sim. *Four Hours in My Lai.* New York: Penguin, 1993.

Birnbaum, Robert. *How Colleges Work.* San Francisco: Jossey-Bass, 1988.

Bliss, Donna, Edward Pecukonis, and Mary Snyder-Vogel. "Principled Leadership Development Model for Aspiring Social Work Managers and Administrators: Development and Application." *Human Service Organizations Management, Leadership & Governance* 38, no. 1 (January 2014): 5–15.

Bohn, Michael. *Heroes & Ballyhoo: How the Golden Age of the 1920s Transformed American Sports.* Sterling, VA: Potomac Books, 2009.

Bordere, X. Jasmine, and Franklin Mixon. "Did Servant-Leadership Save the Lone Survivor? The Pashtunwali Ethos as a Foundation for the Practice of Servant Leadership." *International Journal of Servant Leadership* 14, no. 1 (2020): 359–80.

Boswell, Thomas. "The Game Wasn't Perfect, but the Gentlemen Were." *Washington Post,* June 4, 2010, A01.

Branch, Taylor. *Parting of the Waters America in the King Years 1954–63.* New York: Simon & Schuster, 1989.

Breyer, Stephen. "Airline Deregulation Revisited." *Business Week,* January 20, 2011.

Brinkley, Douglas. *Rosa Parks: A Life.* New York: Penguin, 2005.

Brown, Ian. *A New Conception of War: John Boyd, the U.S. Marines, and Maneuver Warfare.* Quantico, VA: Marine Corps University Press, 2018.

Brown, Michael, Linda Treviño, and David Harrison. "Ethical Leadership: A Social

Learning Perspective for Construct Development and Testing." *Organizational Behavior and Human Decision Processes* 97, no. 2 (July 2005): 117–34.
Cadet Leader Development Program. 3rd ed. Charleston, SC: The Citadel, 2017.
Cambridge Business English Dictionary. Cambridge: Cambridge University Press, 2011.
Catalog of the Citadel 2003–2004. Charleston, SC: The Citadel, 2003.
Chakravarty, Subruta. "Hit 'em Hardest with the Mostest." *Forbes*, September 16, 1991.
Chadwick-Joshua, Jocelyn. *The Jim Dilemma: Reading Race in* Huckleberry Finn. Oxford: University Press of Mississippi, 1998.
Cialdini, Robert. *Influence: Science and Practice.* Needham Heights, MA: Allyn & Bacon, 2009.
The Citadel. *Leader Development Program*. Charleston, SC: The Citadel, 2014.
Collins, James. *Good to Great*. New York: Harper Business, 2001.
Cooke, Alistair. *Alistair Cooke's America.* London: Orion, 2003.
Coram, Robert. *Boyd: The Fighter Pilot Who Changed the Art of War.* Boston: Little, Brown, 2002.
Covey, Stephen. *The 8th Habit: From Effectiveness to Greatness.* New York: Free Press, 2004.
______. *Principle-Centered Leadership.* New York: Fireside, 1992.
______. *The 7 Habits of Highly Effective People.* New York: Simon & Schuster, 1989.
Coyne, Michael. *Hollywood Goes to Washington: American Politics on Screen.* London: Reaktion Books, 2008.
Cross, Frank, and Elizabeth Livingstone, eds. *The Oxford Dictionary of the Christian Church*. 3rd rev. ed. Oxford: Oxford University Press, 2005.
Curry, Scott, Daniel Mullins, and Harvey Whitehouse. "Is It Good to Cooperate? Testing the Theory of Morality-as-Cooperation in 60 Societies." *Current Anthropology* 60, no. 1 (February 2019): 47–69.
Daft, Robert. *The Leadership Experience.* 6th ed. Stamford, CT: Cengage, 2015.
Dalleck, Robert. "JFK vs. the Military." *The Atlantic*, August 2013. https://www.theatlantic.com/magazine/archive/2013/08/jfk-vs-the-military/309496/.
Dantley, Michael. "Principled, Pragmatic, and Purposive Leadership: Reimagining Educational Leadership through Prophetic Spirituality." *Journal of School Leadership* 13, no. 2 (March 2003): 181–98.
Davis, Michael. "The Meaning of Father Damien." *Crisis Magazine*, August 3, 2020.
Delehunt, Anne. "Ashland Oil Inc.: Trouble at Floreffe (A)." *Harvard Business Review*, January 19, 1990.
DeLellis, Anthony. "Clarifying the Concept of Respect: Implications for Leadership." *Journal of Leadership Studies* 7, no. 2 (2000): 35–49.
"Denis Estimon, CEO of We Dine Together, Steps in as New Director of Be Strong." Be Strong. https://bestrong.global/tag/denis-estimon/.
de Volder, Jan. *The Spirit of Father Damien: The Leper Priest—a Saint for Our Time.* San Francisco: Ignatius Press, 2010.
Donadio, Rachel. "Benedict Canonizes 5 New Saints." *New York Times*, October 11, 2009.
Dougherty, Kevin. *Encyclopedia of the Confederacy.* San Diego: Thunder Bay Press, 2010.
______. *Leadership Lessons Learned from the Vicksburg Campaign.* Philadelphia: Casemate, 2003.
Eichinger, Eric. *The Final Race: The Incredible World War II Story of the Olympian Who Inspired* Chariots of Fire. Colorado Springs: NavPress, 2018.
Erikson, Hal. *Any Resemblance to Actual Persons: The Real People Behind 400+ Fictional Movie Characters.* Jefferson, NC: McFarland, 2017.
"Executive Order 10631—Code of Conduct for Members of the Armed Forces of the

United States." National Archives. https://www.archives.gov/federal-register/codification/executive-order/10631.html.

Fabry, Paul. "Carl Lutz Stood Out like a Monument—He Was an Example of What Can Be Done." In *Under Swiss Protection: Jewish Eyewitness Accounts from Wartime Budapest*, edited by A. Hirschi and C. Schallie, 51–66. Stuttgart: Ibidem-Verlag, 2017.

Farrow, John. *Damien the Leper.* New York: Sheed & Ward, 1937.

Fields, Bill. "Golf's Renaissance Legend, Bobby Jones." The Masters, October 21, 2020. https://www.masters.com/en_US/news/articles/2020-10-21/2020-10-21_golfs_renaissance_legend_bobby_jones.html.

Free, Cathy. "Florida High School Students Start Lunch Club So No One Eats Alone: 'Relationships Are Built from across the Table.'" *People*, April 7, 2017. https://people.com/human-interest/florida-high-school-students-start-lunch-club-no-one-eats-alone.

Frieberg, Kevin, and Jackie Freiberg. "20 Reasons Why Herb Kelleher Was One of the Most Beloved Leaders of Our Time." *Forbes*, January 4, 2019.

Galarraga, Armando, Jim Joyce, and Daniel Paisner. *Nobody's Perfect: Two Men, One Call, and a Game for Baseball History.* New York: Atlantic Monthly Press, 2011.

Gandhi, M.K. *An Autobiography or the Story of My Experiments with Truth: A Critical Edition.* New Haven: Yale University Press.

______. *Statement to Disorders Inquiry Committee.* Calcutta: Superintendent Government Printing, India, 1920.

Gardner, John. *On Leadership.* New York: Free Press, 1990.

Garner, Harry. "Developing an Effective Command Philosophy." *Military Review*, September–October 2012, 75–81.

George, Bill. *Discover Your True North.* New York: Wiley, 2015.

Gibb, Ryan. "The Elections in Uganda, February 2016." *African Spectrum* 51, no. 2 (2016). https://journals.sagepub.com/doi/10.1177/000203971605100206.

Glynn, Maryann, and Heather Jamerson. "Principled Leadership: A Framework for Action." In *Leading with Values: Positivity, Virtue and High Performance*, edited by E.D. Hess and K.S. Cameron, 151–71). Cambridge: Cambridge University Press, 2006.

Goldsmith, Marshall. *What Got You Here Won't Get You There: How Successful People Become Even More Successful.* New York: Hyperion, 2007.

Goldstein, Joshua, and Jon Pevehouse. *International Relations.* New York: Longman, 2010.

Goodwin, Doris Kearns. *Team of Rivals: The Political Genius of Abraham Lincoln.* New York: Simon & Schuster, 2006.

Greenleaf, Robert. *Servant Leadership: A Journey into the Nature of Legitimate Power & Greatness.* New York: Paulist Press, 2002.

Grinalds, John. "Developing Leaders at the Citadel." *Command* 47, no. 1 (1998): 6.

Guha, Ramachandra. *Gandhi: The Years that Changed the World; 1914–1948.* New York: Knopf, 2018.

A Guide for the Leader Development Program. Charleston, SC: The Citadel, 2014.

The Guidon. Charleston, SC: The Citadel, 2021.

Halpern, Belle, and Kathy Lubar. *Leadership Presence.* New York: Gotham Books, 2003.

Hendrikz, Karen, and Amos Engelbrecht. "The Principled Leadership Scale: An Integration of Value-Based Leadership." *SA Journal of Industrial Psychology* 45 (March 2019): 1–10.

Holusha, John. "Exxon's Public-Relations Problem." *New York Times*, April 21, 1989. http://www.nytimes.com/1989/04/21/business/exxon-s-public-relations-problem.html?pagewanted=all.

Hook, Steven. *U.S. Foreign Policy: The Paradox of World Power.* 2nd ed. Washington, DC: CQ Press, 2007.

Bibliography

Hunter, James. *The Servant: A Simple Story about the True Essence of Leadership.* New York: Crown Currency, 1998.

Huntington, Samuel. *The Soldier and the State: The Theory and Politics of Civil-Military Relations.* Cambridge, MA: Belknap, 1959.

Institutional Crisis Group. "Uganda's Slow Slide into Crisis." *Africa Report,* November 21, 2017.

International Buddhist Information Bureau. "Thich Quang Do Is Appointed New Leader of the Unified Buddhist Church of Vietnam." August 17, 2008. https://www.europarl.europa.eu/meetdocs/2004_2009/documents/dv/droi_080825_thichquangdo/DROI_080825_ThichQuangDoen.pdf.

"International Hall of Fame Inducts General Edward Katumba Wamala." U.S. Army War College Archives, September 18, 2014. https://www.armywarcollege.edu/News/archives/12425.pdf.

Isidore, Chris. "Southwest Explains Its Meltdown to Congress." CNN.com, February 9, 2023.

Janis, Irving. *Groupthink: Psychological Studies of Policy Decisions and Fiascoes.* Boston: Houghton Mifflin, 1982.

Johansen, Bob. *Leaders Make the Future: Ten New Leadership Skills for an Uncertain World.* Oakland, CA: Berrett-Koehler, 2009.

Johnson, Craig. *Meeting the Ethical Challenges of Leadership.* Los Angeles: Sage, 2018.

Jones, Betty. "Huck and Jim: A Reconsideration." In *Satire or Evasion: Black Perspectives on* Huckleberry Finn, edited by James Leonard, Thomas Tenney, and Thadious Davis, 154–72. Durham, NC: Duke University Press, 1992.

Jones, Bobby. *Golf Is My Game.* New York: Doubleday, 1960.

Jones, Howard. *My Lai: Vietnam, 1968, and the Descent into Darkness.* Oxford: Oxford University Press, 2017.

Journal of the Proceedings of the Constitutional Convention of the State of Alabama, Held in the City of Montgomery, Commencing May 21st, 1901. Montgomery, AL: Brown Printing, 1901.

"Katumba Wamala Shooting: Uganda Minister's Daughter Killed." BBC, June 1, 2021. https://www.bbc.com/news/world-africa-57315083.

Keith, Kent. *Morality and Morale: A Business Tale.* Honolulu: Terrace Press, 2012.

Kelleher, Herb. "The Best Lesson in Leadership." In *Leader to Leader,* edited by Frances Hesselbein and Paul Cohen. San Francisco: Jossey-Bass, 1999.

Kidder, Rushworth. *How Good People Make Tough Choices.* New York: Harper, 1995.

______. *Moral Courage.* New York: William Morrow, 2005.

Kinnier, Richard T., Jerry L. Kernes, and Therese M. Dautheribes. "A Short List of Universal Moral Values." *Counseling and Values* 45, no. 1 (2000): 4–16. https://doi.org/10.1002/j.2161-007X.2000.tb00178.

Klann, Gene. *The Application of Power and Influence in Organizational Leadership.* Fort Leavenworth, KS: CGSC, 2010.

Koehn, Daryl. "Why Saying 'I'm Sorry' Isn't Good Enough: The Ethics of Corporate Apologies." *Business Ethics Quarterly* 23, no. 2 (April 2013): 239–68.

Kouzes, James, and Barry Posner. *The Leadership Challenge: How to Make Extraordinary Things Happen in Organizations.* 5th ed. New York: Wiley, 2012.

Kowitt, Beth. "Southwest's Biggest Mistake Was Forgetting Its Own Culture." *Washington Post,* December 31, 2022.

Lee, Harper. *To Kill a Mockingbird.* Philadelphia: Lippincott, 1960.

Lightner, David. *Asylum, Prison, and Poorhouse: The Writings and Reform Work of Dorothea Dix in Illinois.* Carbondale: Southern Illinois University Press, 1999.

London, Manuel. "Principled Leadership and Business Diplomacy: A Practical,

Values-Based Direction for Management Development." *Journal of Management Development* 18, no. 2 (1999): 170–92.
Lowe, Stephen. *"The Greatest Ever" and a Return to Merion, 1924–1925. Sir Walter and Mr. Jones: Walter Hagen, Bobby Jones, and the Rise of American Golf.* Ann Arbor: Sleeping Bear Press, 2000.
Luttrell, Marcus, with Patrick Robinson. *Lone Survivor.* Large print ed. Farmington Hills, MI: Thorndike Press, 2007.
MacKenzie, Joi-Marie. "High School Senior Creates Group 'We Dine Together' So No Student Has to Eat Alone," ABC News, March 16, 2017, https://abcnews.go.com/Lifestyle/high-school-senior-creates-group-dine-student-eat/story?id=46172969.
Markkula Center for Applied Ethics at Santa Clara University. "A Framework for Ethical Decision Making." https://www.scu.edu/ethics/ethics-resources/ethical-decision-making/a-framework-for-ethical-decision-making/.
Martin, James. *Justice Ignited: The Dynamics of Backfire.* Lanham, MD: Rowman & Littlefield, 2007.
Mataxas, Eric. *Seven Men: And the Secret of Their Greatness.* Nashville: Thomas Nelson, 2016.
McCain, John. *Faith of My Fathers.* New York: Random House, 1999.
______. "John McCain, Prisoner of War: A First-Person Account." *U.S. News & World Report*, January 28, 2008. https://www.usnews.com/news/articles/2008/01/28/john-mccain-prisoner-of-war-a-first-person-account.
McDermott, Rachel Fell, Leonard A. Gordon, Ainslie T. Embree, Frances W. Pritchett, and Dennis Dalton, eds. *Sources of Indian Traditions: Modern India, Pakistan, and Bangladesh.* New York: University of Columbia Press, 2014.
McGlade, Caitlin. "Eating Alone at School: How Four Students Began Mission to End Isolation." *Sun Sentinel*, February 18, 2017. https://www.sun-sentinel.com/news/education/fl-eating-alone-at-school-20170205-story.html.
Menkel-Meadow, Carrie. "Ethics of Compromise." In *Global Encyclopedia of Public Administration, Public Policy, and Governance, edited by* Ali Farazmand. Basel: Springer, 2016. https://www.law.uci.edu/faculty/full-time/menkel-meadow/ethics-as-compromise-Ency.of-Public-Admin-and-Policy.pdf.
Merriam-Webster's Collegiate Dictionary. 11th ed. Springfield, MA: Merriam-Webster, 2020.
Michel, Marshall. "The Revolt of the Majors: How the Air Force Changed after Vietnam." PhD diss., Auburn University, 2006.
"My Lai Rescuer Hugh Thompson Jr." *Washington Post*, January 7, 2016. https://www.washingtonpost.com/archive/local/2006/01/07/my-lai-rescuer-hugh-thompson-jr/29df090b-c47a-4a9c-af0f-6b453ec907bd/.
Mydans, Seth. "Thich Quang Do, 91, Buddhist Monk and Rights Champion in Vietnam." *New York Times*, February 27, 2020.
Nantulya, Paul. "Wisdom from Africa on Ethical Leadership." Africa Center for Strategic Studies, May 9, 2017. https://africacenter.org/spotlight/wisdom-africa-ethical-leadership/.
Neufeld, Jacob. *The F-15 Eagle: Origins and Development, 1964–1972.* Washington, DC: Office of Air Force History, 1974.
Nocera, Joe. "The Sinatra of Southwest Feels the Love." *New York Times*, May 24, 2008.
Norbury, Frank. "Dorothea Dix and the Founding of Illinois' First Mental Hospital." *Journal of the Illinois State Historical Society* 92, no. 1 (Spring 1999): 13–27.
Northouse, Peter. *Leadership: Theory and Practice.* 8th ed. Thousand Oaks: Sage, 2019.
O'Toole, James. "Speaking Truth to Power: A White Paper." Markkula Center for Applied Ethics. https://www.scu.edu/ethics/focus-areas/business-ethics/resources/speaking-truth-to-power-a-white-paper/.

Bibliography

Oxford Advanced Learner's Dictionary. New York: Oxford University Press, 2020.

Paine, Lynn. "Managing for Organizational Integrity." *Harvard Business Review,* March 1, 1994, 106–17.

Pandya, Mukul. *Lasting Leadership.* Upper Saddle River: Prentice Hall, 2005.

Parks, Rosa. *Rosa Parks: My Story.* New York: Puffin, 1999.

Parrish, Thomas. *Roosevelt and Marshall: Partners in Politics and War.* New York: William Morrow, 1989.

Paul, Tony. "10 Years Later, Ex-Tiger Armando Galarraga 'Lucky to Not Be Lucky' in Brush with Perfection." *Detroit News,* June 1, 2020.

Perry, Marion. "Dorothea Dix (1802–1887)." *American Journal of Public Health* 96, no. 4 (April 2006): 624–25.

Pogue, Forrest. *George C. Marshall.* 4 vols. New York: Viking, 1986.

Pojman, Louis, and James Fieser. *Ethics: Discovering Right and Wrong.* Stamford, CT: Cengage, 2011.

Porter, Stanley. "Conflict Resolution: Leadership and the Jerusalem Council." In *Biblical Leadership: Theology for the Everyday Leader,* edited by Benjamin Forrest and Chet Roden, 399–412. Grand Rapids: Kregel, 2017.

Pratley, Gerald. *The Cinema of John Frankenheimer.* New York: Zwemmer/Barnes, 1969.

Prieto, Leon, and Simone Phipps. *African American Management History: Insights on Gaining a Cooperative Advantage.* Bingley, UK: Emerald, 2019.

Prilleltensky, Isaac. "Value-Based Leadership in Organizations: Balancing Values, Interests, and Power among Citizens, Workers, and Leaders." *Ethics & Behavior* 10, no. 2 (2000): 139–58.

Puryear, Edgar. *American Generalship: Character Is Everything; the Art of Command.* Novato, CA: Presidio, 2000.

Quillen, Alanna. "Boca Lunch Club's Mission That No Kid Should Alone Goes Viral." WPTV, March 28, 2017. https://www.wptv.com/news/region-s-palm-beach-county/boca-raton/boca-lunch-clubs-mission-that-no-kid-should-alone-goes-viral.

"Read Rachael Denhollander's Full Victim Impact Statement about Larry Nassar." CNN, January 30, 2018. https://www.cnn.com/2018/01/24/us/rachael-denhollander-full-statement/index.html.

Report of the Department of the Army Review of the Preliminary Investigation into the My Lai Incident. Washington, DC: Department of the Army, March 14, 1970.

Robinson, Jo Ann Gibson. *Montgomery Bus Boycott and the Women Who Started It: The Memoir of Jo Ann Gibson Robinson.* Knoxville: University of Tennessee Press, 1987.

Robinson, Patrick. *The Lion of Sabray.* Kindle ed. New York: Touchstone, 2016.

Rubel, Rick, and George Lucas. *Case Studies in Ethics for Military Leaders.* Boston: Pearson, 2015.

Rubino, John. "Aligning Personal Values and Corporate Values: A Personal and Strategic Necessity." *Employment Relations Today,* Autumn 1998, 23–35.

Safire, William. "On Language: Principles vs Values." *New York Times,* August 12, 1984, section 6, 8.

Schelling, T.C. "Egonomics, or the Art of Self-Management." *American Economic Review* 68, no. 2 (May 1978): 290–94.

Schoenecke, Michael. "Bobby Jones, Golf, and His Instructional Reels." *Film & History* 35, no. 2 (2005): 67–70.

Schwartz, Mark S. "Universal Moral Values for Corporate Codes of Ethics." *Journal of Business Ethics* 50, no. ½ (2005): 27–44. https://www.jstor.org/stable/25123538.

Sendjaya, Sen, James C. Sarros, and Joseph C. Santora. "Defining and Measuring Servant Leadership Behaviour in Organizations." *Journal of Management Studies* 45, no. 2 (March 2008): 402–24.

Shelton, Ken. "Principled Leadership." *Leadership Excellence* 26 (May 2009): 6.

Shillito, Edward. "British Table Talk." *Christian Century* 40, no. 51 (December 21, 1923): 1660.
Simons, Anna. "Backbone vs. Box: The Choice between Principled and Prescriptive Leadership." In *The Future of the Army Profession*, edited by L. Matthews, 379–95. New York: McGraw-Hill, 2002.
"Six UPDF Generals Receive U.S. Legion of Merit Award." U.S. Embassy in Uganda, September 30, 2015. https://ug.usembassy.gov/six-updf-generals-receive-u-s-legion-of-merit-award/.
Smith, T.C. *The Broadman Bible Commentary, vol. 10, Acts–1 Corinthians*. Nashville: Broadman, 1970.
Sorkin, Amy Davidson. "Madame Nhu's Match." *New Yorker*, April 26, 2011. https://www.newyorker.com/news/amy-davidson/madame-nhus-match.
Sterba, James. "POW Commander among 108 Freed." *New York Times*, March 15, 1973.
"Thich Quang Do, Vietnam Dissident Buddhist Monk, Dies at 91." *Washington Post*, February 25, 2020. https://www.washingtonpost.com/local/obituaries/thich-quang-do-vietnam-dissident-buddhist-monk-dies-at-91/2020/02/25/e179c012-5806-11ea-ab68-101ecfec2532_story.html.
Tish, Susan. "A Pitcher, an Umpire, and a Lesson in Grace." *Christian Science Monitor*, June 9, 2010.
Tschuy, Theo. *Dangerous Diplomacy: The Story of Carl Lutz, Rescuer of 62,000 Hungarian Jews*. Grand Rapids: Eerdmans, 2000.
Twain, Mark. *The Adventures of Huckleberry Finn*. New York: Charles L. Webster, 1885.
"Uganda Polls: Museveni's Main Rival, Besigye, Arrested." BBC News, February 19, 2016. https://www.bbc.com/news/world-africa-35612224.
The U.S. Fighting Man's Code. Washington, DC: Office of Armed Forces Information and Education, Department of Defense, 1955.
"Vietnam." United States Center for International Religious Freedom. https://www.uscirf.gov/sites/default/files/Vietnam.pdf.
Wagner, Rodd. "How Herb's Heart Still Beats at Southwest." *Forbes*, January 27, 2019. https://www.forbes.com/sites/roddwagner/2019/01/27/how-herbs-heart-still-beats-at-southwest/?sh=59110c9ecc8e.
Weare, Walter. "Spaulding, Charles Clinton." In *Dictionary of North Carolina Biography*, edited by William Powell, 408. Chapel Hill: University of North Carolina Press, 1994.
Weich, Robert. "Florida High Schooler Ensures Everyone Has Someone to Sit with at Lunch." CBS58, November 25, 2017. https://www.cbs58.com/news/florida-high-schooler-ensures-everyone-has-someone-to-sit-with-at-lunch.
West, Joyce. "John Hall: The Kentucky Commodore." Kentucky Educational Television, April 27, 2016. https://www.pbs.org/video/ket-documentaries-john-hall-kentucky-commodore/.
Wilkins, Sam, and Richard Vokes. *Elections in Museveni's Uganda: Understanding the 2016 Polls*. New York: Routledge, 2018.
Williams, Kenny. "*Adventures of Huckleberry Finn*; or, Mark Twain's Racial Ambiguity." In *Satire or Evasion: Black Perspectives on* Huckleberry Finn, edited by James Leonard, Thomas Tenney, and Thadious Davis, 228–37. Durham, NC: Duke University Press, 1992.
Wilson, Charles Reagan. "Bobby Jones." In *The New Encyclopedia of Southern Culture*, vol. 16, *Sports and Recreation*, edited by Harvey H. Jackson, III, 154–72. Chapel Hill: University of North Carolina Press, 2011.
Wilson, Julian. *Complete Surrender: A Biography of Eric Liddell*. Bletchley, UK: Authentic Media, 2012.
Wisard, François. "Context and Milestones of the Rescue Activities of Carl Lutz and His

Team." In *Under Swiss Protection: Jewish Eyewitness Accounts from Wartime Budapest*, edited by A. Hirschi and C. Schallie, 33–50. Stuttgart: Ibidem-Verlag, 2017.

"Witness Says He Didn't Report Mylai Civilian Deaths to Medina." *New York Times*, August 21, 1971, 9. https://www.nytimes.com/1971/08/21/archives/witness-says-he-didnt-report-mylai-civilian-deaths-to-medina.html.

Wooten, Lynn Perry, and Erika Hayes James. "Linking Crisis Management and Leadership Competencies: The Role of Human Resource Development." *Advances in Developing Human Resources* 10, no. 3 (June 2008): 352–79.

"Years of Arrests and Imprisonments of Mahatma Gandhi." mkgandhi.org.

Yukl, Gary. *Leadership in Organizations*. Upper Saddle River: Pearson, 2010.

Yukl, Gary, and Cecilia Falbe. "Influence Tactics in Upward, Downward, and Lateral Influence Attempts." *Journal of Applied Psychology* 75, no. 2 (1995): 132–40.

Yukl, Gary, Cecilia Falbe, and Joo Young Youn. "Patterns of Influence for Managers." *Group & Organization Management* 18, no. 1 (March 1993): 5–28.

Index

Index

www.ingramcontent.com/pod-product-compliance
Lightning Source LLC
LaVergne TN
LVHW042113070225
803225LV00041B/1097
9781476694818